RESIDENTIAL WORK WITH OFFENDERS

Residential Work with Offenders

Reflexive accounts of practice

EMMA WINCUP
University of Kent at Canterbury, UK

Ashgate

Published by
Ashgate Publishing Limited
Gower House
Croft Road
Aldershot
Hampshire GU11 3HR
England

100374 7063

Ashgate Publishing Company
131 Main Street
Burlington,VT 05401-5600 USA

Ashgate website: http://www.ashgate.com

British Library Cataloguing in Publication Data
Wincup, Emma
    Residential work with offenders : reflexive accounts of
    practice. - (Evaluative research in social work)
    1. Social work with criminals 2. Criminals - Institutional
    care
    I. Title
    364.6

Library of Congress Control Number: 2001098454

ISBN 1 84014 583 8

Printed and bound in Great Britain by MPG Books Ltd, Bodmin, Cornwall

Contents

List of Tables and Figure

Tables

Figure

Acknowledgements

The debts I have incurred in researching and writing this book are numerous. Most of all I am grateful to the four probation areas for granting me access, and to the hostel workers who gave up their time to answer my questions. As none of the hostels are identified, all of these must remain anonymous. Thanks also to Jackie Swift for her efficiency in producing the text. Finally family and friends (academic or otherwise) have provided much needed support as well as welcome distractions. I would like to extend my particular thanks to Amanda Coffey and Ian Shaw for supervising one of the research studies on which this book is based.

1 Introduction

At the beginning of the twenty-first century, writing about working with offenders in a social work series may seem an awkward anomaly. In his address to the 1995 National Probation Conference, Michael Howard (then Home Secretary) refuted the idea that punishment in the community should be equated with social work with offenders. Whilst this view may still have political support, there are some dissenting voices. Butler and Drakeford (2001) suggest that the Probation Service can still be categorised as a social work service operating within the criminal justice system, although they recognise that this is an unfashionable view. I share this view, and note that it is one that continues to be publicly endorsed in Scotland. Social work does not have to be equated with the work of statutory social service departments, and a more inclusive and catholic definition can be adopted which encompasses working with those with welfare needs. Offenders frequently experience a range of well-documented problems including poverty, unemployment, lack of education and training, homelessness, substance use and poor health. These problems warrant social work intervention. Without concerted efforts to address the welfare needs of those who appear before the courts, attempts to influence their offending behaviour will meet with only limited success (Drakeford and Vanstone, 1996a). These welfare 'needs' are increasingly being redefined as 'predictive risk factors' (Worrall, 2001). Criminal justice under the 'new penology' has come to be based on the actuarial principle of risk assessment, in other words attempting to identify, classify and manage groups sorted by level of dangerousness. Thus some offenders are subjected inappropriately to programmes aimed at 'high-risk' offenders rather than seeking to meet their welfare needs through better access to community resources. Attention to managing and assessing risk is essential but to prioritise this aspect of working with offenders over addressing their welfare needs is fundamentally at odds with the new social inclusion agenda. Talking about social work with offenders may be unfashionable, but such talk is badly needed. It lies at the heart of effective practice with offenders, a view frequently espoused by the residential workers I have met since 1995.

1

These residential workers have all been working in approved probation and bail hostels in England and Wales. Despite being in existence for over a century these hostels are a relatively neglected area of the criminal justice system, and for most of their history have received little academic, political or media attention. Their origins and rationale are outlined in detail in the next chapter. It is suffice here to state their current purpose and to highlight some of the distinctive feature of hostels. Their current role is to provide an enhanced level of residential supervision to a wide range of individuals. These include principally bailees, those on probation, and those released from prison on licence. Frequently hostels cater for all these groups thus mixing convicted and unconvicted individuals. This is in contrast to prisons which, at least in theory, try to separate out these categories of prisoners. A further anomaly in terms of criminal justice practice is the mixing of females and males. Hostels are frequently compared to prisons and described as a 'halfway house'. This is because hostel residents are allowed freedom of movement within the restrictions placed upon their lives by the hostel rules and any further conditions imposed on them by the courts (those on bail and on probation) or the Home Office (those on licence).

This book brings together the findings from two research projects conducted between 1994 and 1998. This first was a study of bail hostel provision for women awaiting trial. Through ethnographic methods it aimed to capture the experiences of residents and staff, highlighting the particular needs of female defendants and the ways in which bail hostels aim to offer support. Three hostels were studied: two women-only, and one mixed hostel (mixed in this context refers to accommodation for a small number of women in an otherwise male group, see Wincup, 1996). As with many qualitative studies a mass of rich and detailed data is collected which cannot always be included within the final presentation of the research findings due to time limits or word limits. In this instance I felt that the accounts of the hostel workers had been particularly neglected. A successful application for a small research grant allowed me to revisit this data, and to conduct further interviews with staff working in a men-only hostel. This study explored their particular experiences of conducting residential work with male offenders.

Those who reside in bail and probation hostels are referred to throughout the book as offenders. The term is used largely for simplicity and it is recognised that not all those who reside in approved hostels are convicted offenders.

Research strategies

Qualitative approaches appeared the most congruent with the aims of the initial research. Such approaches are particularly suited to research which is exploratory and stresses the importance of context, setting and the subject's frame of reference (Marshall and Rossman, 1989, p.46). Qualitative data can be collected using a range of methodological techniques and presented to a future audience through meaningful descriptions of how social life is accomplished. Ethnography - defined by Fetterman (1989, p.11) as 'the art and science of describing a group or culture' - was selected because it allows 'an investigator to establish a many-sided and relatively long-term relationship' (Lofland and Lofland, 1984, p.120) with groups of individuals in a natural setting. Specifically, the adoption of an ethnographic approach allowed empathic understanding of criminal justice institutions for women and the lives of the women who live and work in them. The essential characteristics of ethnography are watching what happens, listening to what is said and asking questions. These characteristics resemble the ways in which people make sense of their everyday lives, and this has been regarded as a fundamental strength of ethnography for many social scientists (Hammersley and Atkinson, 1995). Although often used as a term synonymous with participant observation, ethnography is not a research method rather a methodological strategy which applies the particular characteristics described above to researching people's lives for an extended period of time in their own surroundings. Consequently, there is potential to mix methods and contemporary ethnography tends to be multi-method research (Pearson, 1993; Reinharz, 1992; Schatzman and Strauss, 1973). In keeping with this tradition the initial research involved a triangulation of methods including participant observation, semi-structured interviews with hostel staff and residents and documentary analysis.

Following a lengthy series of access negotiations (see Wincup, 1997), three hostels (in three probation areas) initially agreed to participate in the research: a women-only hostel, a women-only hostel with provision for children, and a mixed hostel which accommodated mainly men but had a small annexe with four beds reserved for women. In these hostels, both hostel workers and female residents were interviewed. The interviews were semi-structured in format. Straddling the divide between 'standardised' and 'reflexive' interviewing (Hammersley and Atkinson, 1995), semi-structured interviews allow women to add their own frame of reference and therefore allow interviewers to gain insight into the meanings and interpretations they attach to individual events. They also provide the interview with a clear agenda, allowing particular questions to be asked to ensure comparability and facilitate data analysis. In total, fifteen women residents and fifteen hostel workers were interviewed. The interviews were the main focus of the research project but were supplemented by the use of other research methods; participant observation and documentary research.

Long periods of time were spent participating in the everyday activities of bail hostels. Such activities involved attending meetings, watching television with residents, sharing meals and cups of coffee, shadowing staff and chatting to people as they came in and out of the main office - the hub of hostel activity. These observations were written up in fieldnotes which included descriptions of social processes and their contexts, including the emotional context through which what I observed and experienced as reality was filtered. In addition, a wide variety of documentary records were available to me as a researcher. These included documents produced by individual hostels such as log books in which staff record significant events which have happened in the day, publicity brochures, rules and regulations, policies and documents produced by individual probation services and the Home Office.

The data gathered in the form of interview transcripts, fieldnotes and hostel documents (for example, log books in which key events in the hostel are recorded) provided a strong base for a sociological analysis of the experiences of hostel workers. The data collected through ethnographic fieldwork is voluminous and recalcitrant. After several months in the field, I had amassed fieldnotes, interview transcripts, analytic memos and a variety of documents. Concentrated data analysis began after leaving the field, but as Hammersley and Atkinson (1995) argue, the data analysis process is not a distinct stage in itself. Analysis begins with entry to the field and continues throughout the research. The analysis of the data began with the identification of key themes and patterns. Data was then coded

4

and sorted with the aid of a word-processer rather than a dedicated software package (see Wincup, 1997 for an explanation) in order to organise, manage and retrieve the most meaningful bits of data. Beginning to write was central to the data analysis process. As Coffey and Atkinson (1996) argue, writing is a vital way of thinking about one's data because it makes us think about data in new and different ways and develop analytic ideas.

The methodological approach for the second study was similar. Access was secured to a men-only hostel, and five semi-structured interviews were conducted with staff occupying a variety of roles within the hostel.

The research strategies discussed above may not readily appear as evaluation techniques, nor the research questions as evaluative ones. Greene (1994) notes programme evaluation is frequently oriented around the macro policy issues of effectiveness and cost efficiency. Primary emphasis is placed on effectiveness measured in terms of quantifiable outcomes. Typical evaluation questions are thus: are desired outcomes attained and attributable to the programme?, and is this programme the most efficient alternative? Where possible experimental models are utilised. However, there is a growing interest in qualitative approaches to evaluation. Greene argues that the interpretive turn in the social sciences has allowed approaches to develop which promote pluralism in evaluation contexts, and a case study methodological orientation with an accompanying reliance on qualitative methods. These approaches seek to enhance contextualised understanding for stakeholders closest to the programme such as directors, staff and beneficiaries. The research on which this book is based is an example of an interpretivist evaluation. Its key evaluation question is how was the bail and probation hostel experienced by hostel workers and their managers?

The sample

Four hostels were involved in the two studies. They are referred to in this volume as Victoria House (women-only), Carlton House (women-only with provision for children), North Street Hostel ('mixed' hostel) and Harding House (men-only hostel). Each of the four approved hostels was managed by a senior probation officer who occupied the primary managerial role, although an assistant chief probation officer was ultimately responsible for the work of all approved hostels in each area. A deputy manger was also employed in all four hostels, and with the exception of Victoria House, the post was occupied by a qualified probation officer. Many of the routine day-to-day responsibilities of running the hostels rested with assistant wardens, or project workers as they were known at Victoria House. A Home Office formula determined the actual level of staff, and this was based on the number of bed spaces. In three of the hostels (Victoria House, North Street Hostel and Harding House) dedicated night support workers were also employed. Other staff members varied between hostels, and sometimes included administrative staff, creche supervisors and relief workers. The latter group of staff were usually employed to cover staff absences but were used at Carlton Houses on a regular basis. This was perceived as unacceptable by the manager and potentially risky (see chapter five).

Numerous informal conversations took place with all members of the staff team in each of four hostels, and overall twenty were formally interviewed. These include two managers, four deputy managers, three night support workers and eleven assistant managers. Three-quarters of the sample were in their twenties or thirties, three-quarters of the sample were female, and three-quarters of the sample were white (the remainder were Black or defined themselves as of 'mixed race').

Hostels for offenders: A brief review of the literature

The problem of crime and strategies of crime increasingly receive political, media and public attention. This growing interest is also reflected in the growth of Criminology as an academic discipline which has resulted in a proliferation of research on crime, criminals, victims and criminal justice. Inevitably some areas of criminological interest receive more attention than others. Even when the Probation Service has been the subject of research attention, few studies have looked at hostels, yet this is an important area of criminal justice. Just looking at hostels approved by the Probation Service, there are a total of one hundred hostels which can accommodate approximately 2,260 individuals (Home Office, 2001a). Just over 1,000 staff are employed in hostel on a full-time and part-time basis plus 79 senior probation officers and 80 probation officers (Home Office, 2001b). Increasingly we hear calls from penal pressure groups and penal reformers to consider residential community settings as a response to the ever expanding prison population.

It would unfair to claim that hostels have receive no research attention. Some important studies of hostels have been conducted. A number of Home Office sponsored studies were published in the late 1970s and early 1980s. Much of this work was concerned with the observation and categorisation of hostel regimes. A common theme was to suggest that the warden's style was influential in establishing a regime (Otto and Orford, 1978; Palmer, 1979; Sinclair, 1971), resulting in considerable variations in style between hostels. This is also evident in Fisher and Wilson's (1982) study of two probation hostels which found two contrasting regimes: authoritarian and liberal persuasive. They concluded that an appropriate regime was one based on freedom and authority. Barry (1991) also offered a categorisation of hostel regimes: the rigorous and restrictive, middle of the road and the liberal based on a social work ethos and the upholding of civil rights. This was largely based upon analysis of the restrictiveness of the rules and regulations of twenty-one hostels.

One of the first pieces of work on approved hostels was the evaluation of Field Wing Bail Hostel by Simon and Wilson (1975), at an early stage in the development of bail hostels. Nine months after it opened, their evaluation highlighted tensions between the statutory (Home Office and Probation Service) and the voluntary agencies involved and practical difficulties, but also reported low rates of reoffending, high levels of successful completions and positive feedback from residents. They speculated that many would have been refused bail if hostel places were not available. With the exception of Payne (1989) and Watson (1994), hostels seems to have been overlooked when evaluating probation practice. Payne found two encouraging indicators of success: almost 60% of residents completed their period of residence or were bailed elsewhere (Watson reached a similar figure of 57%), and only 17% of residents received a custodial sentence. Instead, research studies have focused on the utilisation of approved hostels, testing the hypothesis that they are used as an alternative to custodial remands for those whose personal and/or domestic circumstances would otherwise have led them to be remanded in custody (Lewis and Mair, 1989; Pratt and Bray, 1985; White and Brody, 1980). The studies provide information on the characteristics of defendants accommodated in hostels in terms of age, criminal career, housing status, education and work experiences and mental health. Additionally, they provide data about hostels in terms of referrals, selections and breaches of conditions and sentence outcomes. The conclusions arrived at are contradictory. White and Brody (1980) argue that hostels were fulfilling their objectives of diverting defendants away from custody. This is in stark contrast to the research studies by Pratt and Bray (1985) and Lewis and Mair (1988) which suggested that a process of net-widening was in operation. This may be explained by changing political pressures and the development of hostels for those on bail which were officially established by the 1972 Criminal Justice Act, just five years after the research by White and Brody was conducted.

An alternative source of data are the official reports based on hostel inspections. A report (HM Inspectorate of Probation, 1993) based on the findings of a thematic inspection of approved bail and probation hostels examined the role, function and operation of hostels and made recommendations for change. Five years later, a further and more detailed report was published (HM Inspectorate of Probation, 1998). Again, it was based on a thematic inspection which aimed to see whether hostels conformed to the requirements of *National Standards*, Key Performance Indicators outlined in the Three Year Plan (Home Office, 1997) and government expectations. These expectations referred to implementation of the recommendations of the 1993 report and ensuring equality of service provision for women and ethnic minorities. Whilst a useful and up-to-date resource which covers a greater number of hostels than any research study to date, essentially the reports are oriented towards management issues and are largely atheoretical. Like the quantitative studies. the reports do not give a voice to those who live and work in hostels, although the reports claim to have consulted both staff and residents.

There are some examples of work which elucidates actual experiences. These largely takes two forms: practitioner reflection on the realities of hostel work and surveys of residents conducted by individual probation services. Practitioners' accounts have covered issues such as safety (Anon, 1993) and groupwork (Goodwin, 1995; Mulvie, 1993; Sapsed, 1993). To give one example of a survey of residents: Inner London Probation Service conducted a pilot and follow-up survey in 1994 (ILPS, 1994a, 1994b). This was largely based on fixed-response questions, although there was an opportunity for residents to make more lengthy comments on aspects of their experience of living in a hostel. It covered issues such as reception and induction, keyworking, support available, groupwork and experiences of discrimination. From this they concluded that their hostels were not only approved by the Home Office but approved by residents.

Gender has not been totally dismissed in some of the work on hostels to date. Both the 1993 and 1998 inspection reports, particularly the latter, address equal opportunity issues and provision for women. White and Brody (1990) and Pratt and Bray (1985) included a small number of women in their samples, but do not break their statistics down by gender or include any controls for gender. These studies involved the inclusion of a small number of women in the sample, rather than incorporating an analysis of gender. Heidensohn (1997) refers to this as the 'add and stir' approach. Going beyond this approach, Lewis and Mair (1988) compared the problems experienced by female and male residents in a limited way based on hostel records.

Many of the studies to date on hostels have ended with a call for further research. This call still appears valid as many gaps in our knowledge of the operation of hostels remain. This book aims to fill one of those gaps; to document the experiences of twenty individuals who work with offenders in residential settings. The structure of the book is outlined below.

Structure of the book

The remainder of the book is divided into eight chapters. Although intended to be read sequentially, each chapter is relatively self-contained to allow readers, particularly busy practitioners, to dip into the book.

Chapter two offers a critical discussion of the growth of increasingly punitive approaches to crime control within a society which emphasises law and order politics and then go on to examine how this has impacted on probation policy broadly and day-to-day practice with offenders. One key policy change has been the publication of *'National Standards for the Supervision of Offenders in the Community'*, a policy document which provides aims and objectives for all aspects of probation work, including residential work with offenders. *Chapter three* reflects on the compatibility of these national standards with staff expectations of residential work, and considers the problems of translating aims and objectives into practice.

Drawing upon the experiences of workers new to residential work and more experienced workers' recollections of their early days in the field, sociological analyses of the process of becoming a residential worker are presented in *chapter four*. In particular, the chapter reflects upon the development of knowledge, expertise and professional identities, highlights the particular problems experiences by newcomers and suggests ways in which they could be overcome. However, some of the difficulties experienced by those new to residential work are ongoing dilemmas of practice. They include managing risk and danger and coping with stress. These issues are explored in chapters five and six respectively.

Chapter five explores residential workers' accounts of feelings of safety and danger and their strategies for managing risk and vulnerability. It argues that risk permeates every aspect of residential work with offenders and suggests that greater attention to the assessment and management of risk is needed to make residential work with offenders comparable with other forms of probation practice.

Dealing with the risk posed by residents is one source of stress. *Chapter six* examines the different sources of stress experienced by residential workers and their coping strategies. Workers in such setting continually engage in 'emotional labour' which can be stressful but paradoxically can also make residential work stimulating and challenging.

Chapter seven considers the approach developed by residential workers in response to the realities of working with offenders, and examines the ways in which the approach is translated into practice. It focuses on working with women. The findings of this small-scale study are limited in their ability to discuss in detail the experiences of working with men, although there is a short discussion of possible differences between working with women and men at the end of the chapter.

One potential dilemma for hostel workers is reaching an agreement on what constitutes success in relation to residential work with offenders. In *chapter eight* a critique is offered of official measure of the effectiveness of residential work with offenders. Such measures are often quantitative outcome measures. Whilst disregarded by staff as inappropriate ways to evaluate residential work, these measures have significant implications for practice. For instance, these key performance indicators can help to determine available resources and the future existence of individual residential settings. Instead, residential workers stress the need for more complex, qualitative measures which explore the different way in which 'success' can be assessed, grounded within an appreciation of the practicalities of service delivery.

The *final chapter* of the book weaves the strands together and suggests that the combination of working with offenders in residential settings creates a unique blend of dilemmas of practice, and personal difficulties and tensions for workers. Based on the reflexive accounts of those engaged in residential work, possible policy implications are explored. The chapter ends with an assessment of the contribution of qualitative research to evaluations of probation practice and highlights the need for future research.

2 A Century of Residential Work with Offenders

Introduction

This chapter is divided into two parts. The first traces the origins and development of hostels for offenders. Compared to other criminal justice institutions such as prisons or the police, hostels have a relatively short history; existing only since the early part of the twentieth century. Nonetheless, significant changes have taken place during this time which have fundamentally altered their role within the criminal justice system, and this chapter aims to document key changes and map out the most important landmarks. The second part of the chapter focuses on the extent to which a commitment to equal opportunities is enshrined within residential work with offenders, concentrating in particular on issues of gender and inadequate provision for women who offend. The extent to which other client groups such as ethnic minority offenders and mentally disordered offenders are marginalised in terms of hostel provision is also considered.

The research on which this book is based was conducted between 1994 and 1998. These were years marked by great change in relation to criminal justice policy. The Conservative Government tried to convince the electorate that they were the party who could successfully deliver on law and order. What followed was a succession of policies and new legislation which have adopted a punitive stance to crime control, resulting in a ever increasing prison population (Morgan, 2000). New Labour has done little to reverse this trend. May (1991) suggests in his study of the Probation Service that these changes can be analysed at three levels: the macro or environmental level (the changing nature of penal policy), the mezzo or organisation level (changes affecting the Probation Service) and the micro or interactive level (changes in relation to residential work with offenders). Throughout this chapter, changes in relation to residential work with offenders will be discussed against the backdrop of broader shifts in penal policy and their impact on the Probation Service. The historical context will be explored to contextualise present-day debates about crime and its control.

Part One: The origins and development of residential work with offenders

The origins of approved hostels for offenders

The use of hostels to accommodate offenders dates back to the early years of the twentieth century when the Criminal Justice Administration Act (1914) gave the courts powers to add a condition of residence to a probation order. In direct response to this legislative change, a number of charities within the philanthropic movement established hostels for young people. These hostels aimed to offer a disciplined and character building experience (HM Inspectorate of Probation, 1993) for young offenders whose homes were considered to be unsuitable for successful rehabilitation. The first hostels were small, usually accommodating around a dozen residents in dormitories. They were typically managed by male wardens, often with their wives, and were based on an extended family model. Initially, these hostels were run without the support of the Home Office and the criminal justice system. When hostels were being developed the Probation Service was in its infancy, and had yet to expand its duties to cover the management of hostels. Although the Probation Service as we know it today has its origins in the Victorian temperance movement and the police court missionaries who began work in the 1870s and 1880s, it was not until the 1907 Probation of Offenders Act that the Probation Service was put on a statutory footing. By the mid 1920s, the basis of a national bureaucratic machinery was established, laying the foundations for an administrative framework based on probation service areas and introducing more formalised methods of finance, regulation and organisation (Newburn, 1995). Probation officers were now paid employees of a professional body and were required to undergo training. Their work involved supervising hostel residents but hostels continued to be managed and staffed by charitable bodies. Concerned about this ad hoc provision at a time when a more professional criminal justice system was emerging, a Departmental Committee report in 1927 recommended that hostel provision should be expanded and that the Home Office should approve, inspect and fund hostels. At this stage it was not suggested that probation areas should manage and staff hostels. This sea-change was not observed until the 1970s.

The recommendations of the 1927 government report were enshrined in the 1948 Criminal Justice Act, which empowered the Home Secretary to approve and regulate hostels for offenders aged between 15 and 21. It was anticipated that hostels would offer young offenders a stable and supportive environment which catered for their needs and helped them to be reintegrated back into society. This was an era when young people left school at 14 or 15 and jobs or apprenticeships were plentiful. Thus it was expected that residents would be engaged in full-time employment. Indeed, young offenders who lacked the discipline to undertake regular work were sent to 'probation homes' (approved school, farm training schools and public schools) with an emphasis on sport, fitness, regular habits, adventure activity and hard work.

Following the Children and Young Person's Act (1969), probation orders for those under 17 were prohibited. Faced with a reduced group of offenders who could be referred to hostels, hostel provision for adults was introduced. Originally this was instituted on a trial basis. One wing of a Salvation Army hostel in London was utilised as a bail hostel. The purpose behind this initiative was to avoid unnecessary custodial remands of defendants who were likely to abscond if given bail to their home address. This pilot project was evaluated by the Home Office (Simon and Wilson, 1975) and the findings were encouraging (see page 7 for a brief discussion of their findings). Holding on to the belief that initial teething problems could be overcome and acknowledging the positive aspects of the evaluation, Field Wing hostel served as a working model for future developments.

A series of legislative changes in the early 1970s aided the development of hostels for adult offenders. The 1972 Criminal Justice Act empowered the Home Office to finance bail hostels as alternative places of accommodation for people awaiting trial. Probation committees were encouraged to provide bail and probation hostels and other establishments such as day centres which would promote the rehabilitation of offenders. The following year, the Powers of the Criminal Courts Act 1973 made provision for the establishment of approved hostels to be staffed and maintained by the Probation Service. These developments arose not only as a response to the accommodation problems of offenders, but also out of recognition of the fact that they can often be helped more adequately in small institutions which enabled them to remain in employment, to have freedom of movement in the community, and to avoid the dependency and institutionalisation which can come from frequent imprisonment (Haxby, 1978, p.244).

Growing pressures on the penal system and remaining traces of liberalism within penal policy were also influential (Pratt and Bray, 1985). Significantly, the new legislation ended ad hoc hostel provision by the voluntary sector and replaced it with a more co-ordinated and efficient approach with greater input from probation officers in the day-to-day management of hostels. Today most approved hostels are managed and run by the Probation Service. Osler (1995) reports that only fourteen hostels are currently managed by voluntary societies and the remainder by probation committees or boards.

There were further significant developments. In 1976 the Bail Act introduced a presumption in favour of bail, subject to certain exceptions, potentially increasing the pool of possible residents. These exceptions refer to the likelihood that the defendant would fail to surrender to the court, commit further offences, interfere with witnesses or otherwise pervert the course of justice; or if the defendant is in need of protection. This piece of legislation continues to influence bail decision-making although legislative changes in the 1990s have eroded the presumption in favour of bail for certain individuals.[1]

Expansion and contraction: The development of approved hostels

There have been repeated plans to expand hostel provision since their inception. In 1978 the House of Commons Expenditure Committee looked at pressures on the prison system and recommended expansion of the hostel system, particularly for bailees. Following this the numbers of hostels increased slowly. A major expansion programme was planned in the late 1980s. This was a response to overcrowding in prisons, but also to the use of police cells to house remand prisoners which reached an average figure as high as 982 prisoners in 1988. There were plans to create 27 new hostels between 1988 and 1994 which would provide over 1,000 additional bed spaces. Following the 1991 Criminal Justice Act, a commitment to expansion was made again. In February 1992, Kenneth Baker (then Home Secretary) announced the creation of 800 bail beds over three years. This would be backed up by £26 million for capital works and an additional £4-5 million for revenue.

In their attempts to expand the amount of hostel accommodation available, local probation services faced two major obstacles. The first difficulty was the lack of suitable properties for conversion into hostels. The second difficulty, which was far more difficult to overcome, was local opposition. As Worrall (1997a) notes, the NIMBY factor (Not In My Back Yard) meant that planned expansion met with much local resistance as communities expressed concerns about personal safety and potential victimisation. The consequence of these two difficulties was that hostels appeared to be too troublesome an issue and allocated Home Office funds remained unspent (Worrall, 1997a). Where hostels were able to open, they often had to use 'buildings of convenience' and convert them into hostels. In some instances these were inappropriately located, for example near schools, and were frequently described as unsuitable or less than ideal (HM Inspectorate of Probation, 1998). In all four hostels participating in this research, staff repeatedly complained about the unsuitability of their accommodation. Common to all hostels was the problem of 'policing' the building. However, there were also complaints about shared rooms and lack of space for staff to sleep over in comfort and work effectively. Managing relations with the public took up a considerable amount of staff time at Victoria House and North Street Hostel (both were located in residential areas). This was avoided at Harding House because they were located in a busy area which combined commercial and residential buildings and at Carlton House because the hostel was located in its own grounds, set back from the road.

In 1994, the Government took a 'U' turn. Plans to increase hostel provision were abandoned, resulting in many offenders being remanded in custody who might otherwise have been released on bail but for the lack of suitable accommodation (Cavadino and Dignan, 1997). Not only was the expansion programme abandoned but on the 4th April 1994, the Home Office ordered that 11 bail hostels were to close, resulting in a loss of 270 bed spaces or 10 percent of overall provision (Worrall, 1997a). The difficulties of finding suitable premises may have been influential, but the political climate emphasising that 'prison works' and the impact of managerialism emphasising economy, efficiency and effectiveness (see chapter eight) are also central to explaining the Government's actions. As Drakeford and Vanstone (1996a) suggest, prison building was the greatest

16

beneficiary of law and order spending in the 1990s and outside that protected core developments have come to be dominated by the varying climate of public expenditure, 'producing a policy see-saw in which the plans of today are the waste paper of tomorrow' (p.81). Hostels, they note, are the single most prominent example of this. There is a great deal of support for this view although little evidence that the 'see-saw' is moving towards the expansion of hostels again. Overall between 1993 and 1997, 15 hostels closed resulting in a loss of 411 beds. Closures were due to unsuitability, failure to meet Home Office occupancy targets and lack of economic viability (HM Inspectorate of Probation, 1998). Whilst the reduction of hostel accommodation in the face of an explicit commitment to expansion is of great concern, the consequences of the closures are in some ways less dramatic than they first appear. This is because closure was accompanied by greater use of hostel accommodation that was already available. Thus whilst the number of bed spaces available fell from 2655 in 1993 to 2224 in 1997, the average number of bed spaces occupied marginally increased from 1805 in 1993 to 1845 in 1997. Nonetheless, from 1993 the prison population began to increase and the failure of the expansion programme can be regarded as a missed opportunity for diverting some offenders from custody and easing the pressures of overcrowding on the prison estate.

Current provision (NAPO, 2000) stands at 99 hostels. Hostels now tend to be generic (accommodating both convicted and unconvicted offenders) rather than specialist. Since 1974, bailees can be accommodated in probation hostels. This standards in stark contrast to the prison system which aims to segregate these two groups as far as the possible. The vast majority accommodate residents on bail and probation, as well as a range of other resident groups including prisoners on temporary release, those released from prison on licence and those undergoing a bail assessment.[2] The exception to this shift towards generic provision are the small number of hostels which cater for specific resident groups, for example mentally disordered offenders (one hostel) and women (four hostels), in two cases offering provision for their children as well. Provision for these groups is discussed in more detail in part two of this chapter.

Table 2.1   Current provision in approved hostels

Type of hostel	Gender of residents	Number of hostels
Probation and Bail	Men	53
Probation and Bail	Women	4
Probation and Bail	Men and Women	36
Bail	Men	3
Bail	Men and Women	3

Source: NAPO (2000)

The recent history of approved hostels

The development of hostels coincided with a broader concern with the impact of social factors, particularly housing and employment, on offending. It was felt that hostels could cater for the welfare needs of offenders through offering them stable accommodation, and support with move-on accommodation and finding employment. It was anticipated that this level of support and stability would enable offenders to complete their probation order without offending and facilitate their rehabilitation.

The role of bail and probation hostels has undergone a number of dramatic changes during their short history and these are succinctly summarised by Worrall (1997a).

> With high levels of unemployment and the demand for provision to keep more serious offenders out of prison, especially while on remand between court appearances, the probation hostel has become less of a roof over one's head and more a house of correction in its own right.
>
> (Worrall, 1997a, p.107)

Hostels have lost their original rationale of providing temporary accommodation for young petty offenders who went to work during the day. Levels of homelessness and housing problems remain high amongst offenders (Carlen, 1990, 1996; Paylor, 1995; Stewart, 1996) and whilst hostels have an important role to play in providing stable accommodation,

18

the official view is that hostels should be used only for those who require an enhanced level of residential supervision (Home Office, 2000). Residents who go out to work are now the rare exception rather than the norm. High levels of unemployment, particularly amongst those with criminal convictions (Crow, 1996), have reduced opportunities for work amongst hostel residents. In some cases, finding work is often inappropriate due to difficulties such as problem substance use or poor health.

Changes in the nature of the work undertaken in hostels coincided with broader changes in the nature of probation work. In little more than a century, the Probation Service has developed from being a localised, voluntary, evangelical outreach provision to being a profession whose work is integral to the criminal justice system through its work with 'high risk' offenders (Worrall, 1997a). The 1991 Criminal Justice Act, motivated by a concern with prison overcrowding and a belief that community penalties were regarded by sentencers and the public as 'soft' options, aimed to provide a new coherent sentencing framework based on the principles of just deserts. Endorsing the role of community penalties in the criminal justice system, the aim of this new legislation was to reserve imprisonment for only the most serious of offences and elsewhere use an expanded range of community punishments. Of particular significance for the work of the Probation Service was the conversion of the probation order into a 'sentence' or 'punishment', allowing it to be combined with other penalties even for the same offence. The 1991 Act embodied the new approach which the Probation Service had been gradually exposed to throughout the 1980s. In 1984, the Home Office issued a *Statement of National Priorities and Objectives* (Home Office, 1984) which directed it to focus more exclusively on 'high tariff' offenders for whom the risk of custody is greater. A Green Paper published in 1988 (Home Office, 1988) signalled the clear determination of the Home Office to define probation in terms of punishment and control (Cavadino and Dignan, 1997). Moreover, intensive supervision, encouraged by a Home Office Action Plan was introduced, particularly for high-tariff young adult offenders (Mair et al, 1994). Many of the measures introduced in the 1991 Act were subverted as the penal climate grew colder and knee-jerk reactions to 'teething problems' produced new and increasingly punitive legislation[3] (Worrall, 1997a).

The 1991 Act also had an impact on hostels. Whilst approved hostels are still used for those on probation, they can only accommodate those charged offences deemed serious enough under the terms of the 1991 Criminal Justice Act (Osler, 1995). Coupled with this a growing remand population in the early 1990s has resulted in a change of direction for approved hostels. The female remand population has risen consistently since 1993 and the latest data available show that it is continuing to rise (Home Office, 2001c). The average number of men on remand increased between 1992 and 1994, falling in 1995 and rising again at the end of the twentieth century. The most recent data report a small decrease in the male remand population (Home Office, 2001c). In the early 1990s pressures on the prison estate led to the unsatisfactory use of police cells for remand prisoners although this measure has not been taken since 1996. As a consequence, approved hostels now tend to be used for those on bail. In 1997, less than 22 percent of hostel places were occupied by residents subject to a probation order with over 65 percent of beds occupied by bailees. Hostels are now required to be selective in their admissions, rejecting anyone whose offence is too minor, who might harm staff or other residents or who are vulnerable to harm from other residents. Strict rules operate prohibiting disruptive or offensive language and violent and abusive behaviour. Worrall (1997a) notes that whilst this is reasonable in theory and hostels should insist on a standard of civilised behaviour, one consequence is that those most in need of the support offered by hostels are increasingly excluded because of the high standards they are required to reach before admission.

The original ethos of the Probation Service to 'advise, assist and befriend' has know been replaced with 'confront, control and monitor' (Worrall, 1997a). There have been considerable challenges to probation's social work base and probation is now experiencing a crisis of identity (Buchanan and Millar, 1995, 1997; Drakeford and Vanstone, 1996b). Pertinent to this are the distancing of probation training from social work education, a growing emphasis on punishment in the community and the glossing over of the social context of offending. Some of these changes fundamentally conflict with social work values, others have shifted the delicate balance between care and control (Buchanan and Millar, 1997). The tension between care and control has been commented upon by other writers on the Probation Service (Boswell, 1989; Fielding, 1984; Mathieson, 1992; Newburn, 1995). The dilemma of care and control is perhaps heightened in hostels. Although hostels have a duty to serve the courts, they need also to be aware of the unconvicted status of many of their residents.

Coupled with the change of ethos has been the move towards centrally determined prescriptivist practice as part of the march of managerialism (see chapter eight). The Home Office has increasingly begun to exert control over probation areas which had traditionally adopted a laissez-faire approach. A series of developments included the publications including *Statement of National Objectives and Priorities* (1984); *Crime, Justice and Protecting the Public* (1990); *Supervision and Punishment in the Community* (1990); *Partnership in Dealing with Offenders in the Community* (1990) and *Organising Supervision in the Community* (1991) influenced probation management and policy (Worrall 1997a). The publication of *National Standards for the Supervision of Offenders* in 1992 (modified in 1995 and again in 2000) is frequently perceived as impinging on the professional autonomy of 'grassroots' probation officers in all aspects of their work. Commonly referred to as *National Standards*, this publication defines the purpose of approved hostels, specifies rules, outlines an admissions policy, outlines supervisory and enforcement practice, describes requirements for recording information and sketches arrangements for electronic monitoring. These will be discussed in further detail in chapter three.

Looking towards the future

The most recent HM Inspectorate of Probation (1998) report based on a thematic review of approved hostels highlighted three issues worthy of consideration to enable approved hostels to enhance their contribution in the future. Firstly, it notes that the development of hostels nationwide has been piecemeal and recommends a national strategy which would determine what form of provision is needed, how that could best be provided and where it should be located. As we have discussed in this chapter, the development of approved hostels has been sporadic. This has resulted in some areas still having relatively few hostels, for instance Wales and the South West. The development has been strongest in concentrated centres of population such as London, the West Midlands and Greater Manchester and this is not always compatible with the demand for places. Initially this was not problematic as the guiding philosophy was that offenders should be moved away from their homes in the hope that a new environment will enable them to deal effectively with their problems (Osler, 1995). However, there is now a tendency to keep those who offend near their homes as it recognised that preserving family ties and forging links with outside support agencies can help to prevent offending (Light, 1993; Woolf 1991). This mirrors the response to other groups in need of residential care, for example, problem substance users (Wincup et al, 1998). Due to funding arrangements, probation areas generally prefer to use hostels within their own area although some of the more specialist hostels such as those for women or mentally disordered offenders are actively promoted as national resources.

As a consequence of the way hostels have developed in a rather sporadic fashion, initially without national guidance, hostels vary in terms of the facilities they provide to residents. Both the 1993 and 1998 inspection reports are littered with references to services being 'varied', 'ranging between' or 'inconsistent'. Thus the inspectors strongly recommend that steps are taken by the Home Office to rectify the inequitable provision of services across hostels. The introduction of *National Standards* may have eradicated some, but perhaps not all, of this variation. One way forward is to advocate the introduction of minimum standards to ensure anti-discriminatory practice. The danger attached to this approach is that local probation services, faced with cash-limited budgets, may fail to improve on these minimum standards and in some cases hostels may close if these cannot be achieved.

Finally, the Inspectors question the greater use of hostels for bailees rather than those on probation and asks whether this reflects the most effective use of an expensive resource intended to provide an enhanced level of supervision. Whilst it is recognised that hostels could be used appropriately for high risk offenders such as those released from prison, and some hostel staff felt that in the future their work would be with this group, there is a strong argument for using hostels for those awaiting trial who need the support and structure hostels can provide and would otherwise be remanded in custody. However, the research evidence on whether hostels are actually diverting offenders from pre-trial custody is mixed. White and Brody (1980) argue that hostels are fulfilling their objectives and accommodating those at risk of custody but this contrasts with the research studies by Pratt and Bray (1985) and Lewis and Mair

(1989) who suggest there is some evidence of net-widening. They reach similar conclusions.

> Although in a significant number of cases the hostel clearly was diverting residents from custody, it seemed that a number might have been bailed to the hostel unnecessarily and were therefore taking up places which could have been used for those in more critical need of them.
>
> (Pratt and Bray, 1985, p.171)

> [I]n many cases (though probably not the majority) those remanded to hostels would not – or should not – have been remanded in custody. For example, hostels may be used to provide support for those perceived as presenting serious social problems, and this may be more likely in the case of female defendants.
>
> (Lewis and Mair, 1989, p.40)

Throughout the research, hostel staff argued that hostels were cost-effective when compared to the cost of imprisonment. Figures published by NACRO (1995) state the average cost of a prison sentence per week is £437 compared to £284 for a period of residence in an approved hostel. Faced with scarce resources and the need to divert offenders from overcrowded prisons, one solution may be to experiment with privatisation. This has already been introduced in other areas of criminal justice including prisons and policing as part of the broader privatisation movement. Indeed there is already a precedent of community penalties being managed by the private sector, particularly electronic monitoring or 'tagging'. The idea of privatisation in relation to hostels has already been mooted.

> There were also plans in the early 1990s expansion programme to put bail/probation hostels out to tender, potentially privatising them through encouraging the involvement of voluntary and private sectors.
>
> (Newburn, 1995)

Arguments for and against privatisation have been discussed elsewhere (Drakeford, 2000; Sparks 1996) Whilst not advocating privatisation, certainly there appears to be a sense of inevitability amongst practitioners that privatisation will impact on residential work with offenders.

Probation is likely to be caught up in the moves that are affecting many public bodies - privatisation, agency status, buying in services and short-term contracts ... Hostels and community services may well be run by other agencies.

(John O'Sullivan, Senior Probation Officer, quoted in Osler, 1992, p.164)

News that one of the largest bail hostels in London is to be tested - to see whether a voluntary or private sector partners could provide or run an approved hostels to at least the same standard at lower cost - suggests that the above speculation is a likely outcome (Prison Reform Trust, 1999).

Part Two: Equal opportunities?

Equality of opportunity is a notion that gained popularity in the UK in the 1980s and has led to the development of equal opportunities policies governing many areas of social life. One problem is conceptualising what is actually meant by the term equality of opportunity. The concept embraces a multitude of beliefs, expectations, attitudes and practices (Dominelli, et al, 1995). Equality is often defined simplistically as parity of treatment. This definition is adopted in *National Standards*. In this document, equal opportunities only get a brief mention, confined to one bullet point in the introduction.

The National Standards, called "the standards" are predicated on the principle that all services, and organisations acting on their behalf, will operate fairly and consistently to all offenders and avoid discrimination on grounds of race, nationality, ethnic origin, sex, age, disability, religion, sexual orientation or any other improper ground.

(Home Office, 2000, p.1)

Parity of treatment may not lead to fairness in practice. This debate has been particularly advanced in relation to the treatment of female offenders by the courts (Allen, 1987; Eaton, 1986; Kennedy, 1992; Worrall, 1995). The common theme within these writings is that there is a need to recognise the particular social injustices which some groups experience, and appreciate that these cannot be overcome through conventional equal opportunities policies. Treating equally people who are unequal may create further inequality. These commentators suggest that what is needed is

24

unequal treatment, in other words a fair and unbiased appraisal of each person and their situation, without relying on preconceived notions and a conscious decision to target resources for special provision for these groups. Thus equal opportunities policies should take account of the specific issues and specific areas of need in relation to women, ethnic minorities and other marginalised groups.

As they stand, equal opportunities policies tend to focus on the structure of criminal justice agencies; for example examining recruitment and promotion practices and provision for groups of offender and victims. In other words then confine themselves to access issues, limiting themselves to a small segment of the framework of oppression and focusing on issues of quantity rather than quality (Dominelli et al, 1995). Monitoring under Section 95 of the 1991 Criminal Justice Act is a good example of this because of its focus on outcomes rather than the process of criminal justice. Whilst this is a important aspect of change, there is a need to consider the culture of agencies in order to create a climate where everyone feels comfortable, respected and valued. Grimwood (1995) suggest that the essence of equality of opportunity is accepting and welcoming diversity and this requires gradual rather than dramatic cultural change. Discriminatory attitudes still pervade the criminal justice system and whilst the Probation Service may not posses the equivalent of 'cop culture' (Fielding, 1994; Reiner, 2000), studies have exposed evidence of sexism and racism (Allen, 1987; Denney, 1992; Gelsthorpe, 1992; Minogue, 1994).

A gendered agenda?

Does the Probation Service have a gendered agenda? This is a deliberately ambivalent question. In one sense, it asks whether a concern with gender issues has been taken on seriously by the Probation Service so that a commitment to equality of opportunity permeates the work it does? In another sense, it asks a more negative question: is the Probation Service agenda a male-oriented agenda, driven by the needs of male offenders and taken forward by (predominantly male) managers.

Women and men occupy different roles in the Probation Service and there is evidence of both horizontal and vertical segregation.[4] As at 31st December 1999, women made up 61 percent of probation officers and 44 percent of probation officers above main grade were women. Looking in more detail at the roles women occupy reveals that women are over-represented in non-probation officer grades, especially clerical and administrative positions; and under-represented in management probation officer grades. Interestingly, hostel workers are more likely to be women than men, despite the fact that most hostels are for male offenders.[5] On 30th June 1996, women comprised 55 percent of those working within hostels, excluding qualified officers (Home Office, 1997). Merchant (1993) suggests that this may be to do with it being seen traditionally as a predominantly caring role. However, it may also reflect women's lack of access to training opportunities due to commitments in the private sphere.

Table 2.2   Percentage of women employed by grade (30th June 1999)

Grade	Percentage of women employed
Chief Probation Officer	30
Deputy Chief Probation Officer	38
Assistant Chief Probation Officer	32
Senior Probation Officer	45
Probation Officer	59
Non Probation Qualified	76

Source: Home Office (2001b)

A number of authors have suggested that as a consequence of women's under-representation in senior positions, the value-base of the Probation Service is symptomatic of a male-dominated organisation in which the marginalisation of women staff is reflected in the marginalisation of service delivery to women. (Merchant, 1993; Wright and Kemshall, 1994). Probation Service provision for women can be characterised in three ways and these are explored in detail below.

1   Neglect and marginalisation

Two recent studies funded by the Home Office (Hedderman and Gelsthorpe, 1997) highlighted the reluctance of sentencers to fine women which sometimes led to them being discharged and at other times to them being given a more serious community penalty. The most commonly used community penalty was the probation order because magistrates tended to regard female offenders as troubled and therefore wanted to assist them rather than punish them. This well-intentioned action can have serious implications for women if they re-offend or breach their orders and in any case, it is fundamentally flawed because of the lack of appropriate provision for women (HM Inspectorate of Probation, 1996).

In 1991, Probation Service provision for women offenders (HM Inspectorate of Probation, 1991) was reviewed. The report concluded that women offenders were not dealt with in the same way as men by the Probation Service. Women were sometimes precluded, inadvertently, from the full range of community penalties because providing appropriate supervision for the small numbers of women on community sentences was not economically viable. In addition, community service was seen as a 'macho' environment with the hours of attendance being potentially disruptive to the domestic responsibilities of women. Five years later, a similar review was conducted (HM Inspectorate of Probation, 1996). The inspectors found that only a minority of probation areas had strategies, action plans or practice guidelines to help ensure that women had equal access to community sentences and only a minority provided women-only group work and community service tasks. The complexities of women's lives as offenders, but also as partners, parents and victims, were appreciated but often this knowledge was not translated into gender-sensitive pre-sentence reports, partnership arrangements regarding substance use and unemployment or appropriate evaluations of practice.

A recent analysis of community service provision for women by Worrall (2000) concluded that there was a lack of will to develop appropriate and imaginative community service projects for women and together with seeming complacency about women on probation contributes to the unnecessary expansion of the prison estates. She argues that:

> At a time when the Prison Service is finally paying attention to the needs of women in custody, it is unacceptable that the Probation Service seems unclear about service delivery to women offenders in the community.

> (Worrall, 2000, p.11)

2   *The novelty factor*

Women make up only 12 percent of clients supervised by the Probation Service (Home Office 1999). Consequently, pressure from large numbers of male offenders drives the planning of resources and often leads to the particular needs of female offenders being glossed over. Female probation clients are seen as the exception rather than the norm. This perception emerged during the fieldwork.

> You tend to get probation officers who become very involved with the women because they don't get many on their case load and it's a bit of a novelty.
>
> (Manager, Carlton House)

Whilst this can lead to some positive outcomes, for example more detailed pre-sentence reports, there are some negative consequences as Walker describes below.

> Numbers of female probation clients are relatively small and most probation officers will have few on their caseloads. This may reinforce the tendency to deal with women clients as exceptional or abnormal rather than reaching a broader understanding from studies of female offenders and shared information as a team.
>
> (Walker, 1985, p.68)

3   Good practice

A number of authors have attempted to outline what constitutes good practice in working with women (Ablitt, 2000; Buckley and Wilson, 1989; Rumjay, 1996; Wright and Kemshall, 1994). These authors argue for a woman-centred approach which acknowledges the constraints gender roles place upon women and the realities of their lives. There are some example of probation practice which maybe termed woman-centred. Examples include groupwork for women (Goodwin, 1995; Hay, 1998; Hirst, 1996; Jones et al, 1993. Mistry, 1993; Thomas, 1993). Such practices are not widespread. The 1996 Inspection report (HM Inspectorate of Probation, 1996) found that that the priority given to providing quality services to women offenders varied between areas and whilst some services had begun to develop their facilities, others had not. Wright and Kemshall's (1994) research sheds some light on the reasons for this variation. They note that feminist initiatives in the Probation Service have too often relied upon the energy, enthusiasm, commitment and determination of a few interested individuals. Whilst such efforts have placed gender on the agenda, this is insufficient to sustain them in the long-term. Of significance here is Worrall's (1998) argument that the abolition of the requirement for probation officers to have a social work qualification has indirectly masculinised the service and one implication of this will be to reduce the number of female officers with a particular commitment to working with female offenders. Next, we will focus open the implications of the gendered agenda for women seeking hostel accommodation.

Hostel provision for women

At present, women requiring hostel accommodation in the sector approved by the Probation Service can be referred to one of four women-only hostels or one of the thirty-nine mixed hostels in England and Wales (NAPO, 2000). These mixed hostels stand in stark contrast to the traditional tendency to segregate females and males in the criminal justice system. They predominantly accommodate male bailees and/or probationers, but reserve a small number of beds for females. Previous reports by the Probation Inspectorate (HM Inspectorate of Probation, 1993) have argued that this is an unsatisfactory arrangement, particularly the practice of accommodating lone females in a predominantly male hostel. Instead, they have advocated the use of specialist resources such as women-only hostels. A major difficulty here is that the small number of women requiring hostel accommodation leads to the provision of few resources, and hence many women are accommodated at long distances from their homes, families or communities. For these reasons, the few resources that are available are sometimes under used.

The Inspectorate found that hostel accommodation for women was patchy and poorly co-ordinated with few opportunities for women to stay with their children. Although requested, few services volunteered information about the support offered to women in mixed hostels, if they were dealt with differently or whether there were training programmes especially arranged for them. Two years later, a thematic review of hostels was published (HM Inspectorate of Probation, 1998). Again the patchy provision for women was noted and concerns were expressed by residents and staff in mixed hostels relating to privacy, safety, lack of separate facilities and male-oriented programmes and activities were noted. They suggested that there was a strong case for arguing that the present practice of accommodating very small numbers of women in mixed hostels was unsatisfactory. At the same time, they noted that a viable number of women residents could lead to appropriate work being done with them in a supportive atmosphere which was conducive to tackling offending behaviour and meeting their needs. There appears no commitment to furthering the development of women-only hostels or putting safeguards in place to improve provision in mixed hostels. The net result is that few women are diverted from custody into appropriate supportive environments.

The adequacy of current provision was explored with both residents and staff (see Wincup, 1996 for a more detailed discussion). The main theme which emerged from the accounts of staff was that mixed hostels present a number of difficulties in terms of ensuring the privacy, safety and equality of service for their female residents, particularly when female residents are very much in the minority. As hostel workers in the mixed hostel commented:

> I think this is the worst set up you can have and I do think the women
> lose out, but some women in the hostel do make it a success.
>
> (Assistant manager, North Street Hostel)

Talking to the women in the mixed hostel showed their determination to make it a success. They, like some of the women in the women-only hostels, maintained that they preferred a mixed environment. Other were strongly opposed. In general, women tended to prefer the type of hostel accommodation they were in, but this was not always the case. There is a clear need for flexibility in the system, allowing, where practical, all defendants to express their preferences in terms of hostel accommodation: whether mixed, women-only or male-only. The need for choice was stressed by hostel workers too. Presenting choices could be beneficial in helping hostels to achieve their goal of providing a supportive and structured environment, and encouraging successful completions.

Issues of race and ethnicity

Following the death of Stephen Lawrence and the subsequent MacPherson Report, tackling racism is high on the criminal justice agenda. The Probation Service has long been committed to anti-racist initiatives but there are ongoing concerns that black workers and their clients are responded to in stereotypical and discriminatory ways (Denney, 1992;

30

Dominelli et al, 1995). The over-representation of Afro-Caribbean offenders in prison and their under-representation on community sentences is a well-rehearsed problem (Worrall, 1997b).

Hostel provision for black and other ethnic minority offenders is inadequate (Worrall, 1997a). The 1993 HM Inspectorate of Probation report found that only 21 out of 207 residents in the 12 hostel inspected were from ethnic minority communities. This was attributed to a low number of referrals relating to ethnic minority clients. A report five years later (HM Inspectorate of Probation, 1998) found similarly low number: only 10 percent of residents were from ethnic minority group, and this figure is still accurate (Home Office, 2001b). Ethnic minorities are over-represented in hostels when compared to their proportion in the general population (5.5 percent at the time the 1991 census was conducted). However, ethnic minorities make up 18 percent of the male prison population and 24 percent of the female prison population and some of these prisoners may be potential hostel residents (Home Office, 1999).

There are a number of reasons for the low rate of referrals of ethnic minorities. Hostel staff suggested to the 1993 inspectors that hostels may be perceived as 'white institutions' which are unresponsive to the needs of ethnic minority offenders. This perception may be held by offenders and referrers but it seems unlikely that hostels are perceived as more culturally insensitive than the alternative which is frequently custody for bailees. Another explanation relates to discrimination in the courts. Roger Hood's (1992) research based on five Crown Courts in the West Midlands found that black defendants were more likely to be remanded in custody and later given a custodial sentence and this was attributed to discrimination rather than an equal application of bail and sentencing criteria.

The Commission of Racial Equality has expressed reservations about separate provision for black people (Commission for Racial Equality, 1990) and instead promotes the development of anti-racist strategies and practice in hostels to ensure the full range of provision is available to black people. The report powerfully states that the creation of hostels for ethnic minorities as a solution to harassment and racism in hostels amounts to an abrogation of responsibilities. However, it does not rule out consideration of the development of ethnic minority single-sex hostels. Whilst steps have to be taken to respond more consistently and actively to the needs of ethnic minority offenders, there remains considerable scope for further improvements. As in other areas of anti-discriminatory practice, hostel staff are cautious about making any claims that they are successfully catering for ethnic minority residents and this laudable introspection may result in more and more ethnic minorities being sent to prison (Worrall, 1997a). A study undertaken in 1996 (Todd, 1996) suggests that a more culturally sensitive service can be offered to ethnic minority residents if attention is given to the following: reviewing referral and admissions systems, forging links with ethnic minority agencies, developing anti-discriminatory practice training, increasing the employment of black staff, supporting ethnic minority provision and creating or improving a multi-cultural environment. However, the responsibility for ensuring that hostels are accessible to ethnic minorities who appear before the courts does not rest solely with hostel staff but with the Probation Service and the courts. Whilst access to hostels as an alternative to custody should be promoted, care needs to be taken to ensure that ethnic minority offenders are not accommodated in hostels inappropriately.

Further evidence of marginalisation: Mentally disordered offenders and offenders with disabilities

The impact of community care policies has been felt sharply in approved hostels. A significant number of people with mental disorders who would previously have been patients within psychiatric hospitals were now being referred to approved hostels. This group of residents pose major difficulties for both hostel staff and other residents. Mentally disordered residents themselves are at risk of being bullied or victimised by other residents and are not always able to gain access to appropriate medical care and support in the community (HM Inspectorate of Probation, 1998). Insufficiently trained hostel staff were therefore trying to work with this challenging client group and were reliant on collaborative arrangements with local psychiatric services. At Victoria House, a psychiatrist visited the hostel on a weekly basis to work with women with mental disorder, as well as mental illnesses and personality disorder. The probation area which managed Carlton House had established multi-agency collaboration through a partnership initiative with a regional secure unit and regional forensic psychiatric services.

There is one example of an approved hostel which offers a specialist service, targeting offenders with mental disorders (Brown and Geelan, 1998). Elliott House in the West Midlands is run in conjunction with a local forensic psychiatric service. It caters for all types of male offenders who are unable to access to hospital treatment because their mental disorder is not sufficiently acute. Rehabilitation in a medical sense is not offered but the hostel aims to break the circle of imprisonment, reoffending and deteriorating mental health. A recent evaluation (Griffin et al, 1997) notes how the partnership approach facilitates appropriate and cost-effective provision. Elliott House accommodates up to twenty men and is a national resource. No equivalent exists for women although HM Inspectorate of Probation (1998) recommended that a feasibility study should be undertaken.

Access for disabled offenders remains limited despite attempts to repair and refurbish buildings. The major obstacle is the lack of purpose built accommodation. As discussed previous in this chapter, buildings used were often designed for other purposes and are not ideal for conversion into approved hostels. Consequently it was particularly difficult to accommodate offenders with mobility problems.

The way forward?

The above discussion suggests a number of implications for practice. At a general level, a commitment to recognising the needs of particular groups of offenders is required and should form the basis of a client-centred approach in all forms of hostels and in probation practice generally. This raises issues for training, ensuring all staff have access to awareness raising courses and anti-discriminatory training. Clear policy statements are also required which identify and underpin the principles of equality in relation to work with offenders. More specifically, work is need to overcome potential discriminatory practices and to promote the inclusion of excluded groups. To develop an approach which recognises the particular needs of excluded groups requires sufficient resources to be devoted towards allowing workers to develop appropriate programmes and facilities.

Merchant (1993) raises a key issue in her discussion of equal opportunities at a conference focusing on gender. She suggests that although it is important to work on discrete equal opportunities issues relating to race, gender, sexual orientation, disability and other interest groups, there is also a need to integrate all forms of equal opportunities work within a wider anti-discriminatory framework. In order to promote anti-discriminatory practice, a collective commitment to change is required at the level of practice, organisation and structure (Wright and Kemshall, 1994) and personal, institutional and cultural (Dominelli et al, 1995). Only through concerted efforts can the commitment to equal opportunities stated in *National Standards* move from rhetoric to reality.

Notes

1. The relevant legislation is the 1993 Bail Amendment Act, 1994 Criminal Justice and Public Order and 1998 Crime and Disorder Act (see Ashworth, 1998). The Human Rights Act 1998 is likely to have a significant impact on current pre-trial practices (Brookman et al, 2001).

2. Defendants who are being considered for non-custodial sentences will often be bailed to a hostel for an assessment period, usually lasting four weeks. This 'bail assessment' period is after conviction but prior to sentencing. During that time the hostel decides whether or not to offer a place for the defendant to live at the hostel on a condition of residence as part of a probation order.

3. Mostly notably the 1994 Criminal Justice and Public Order Act and 1997 Crime (Sentences) Act.

4. Horizontal segregation describes the tendency for women and men to be concentrated in different types of work. Vertical segregation refers to women's under-representation at the top of the occupational hierarchy in a profession.

5. Hostels for women-only only employ women which is permitted under the 1976 Sex Discrimination Act.

3 Rhetoric and Reality: Working within the Framework of *National Standards*

> I'm quite happy about national standards – I haven't known anything else – but I hope that they do not become excessively demanding as this will make life very difficult for us and they will ultimately be unhelpful to offenders and the community.
> (Karen Grenhalgh, recently qualified probation officer who began her career as a hostel worker, quoted in Osler, 1995, p.170)

Introduction

In the previous chapter we explored the history of residential work with offenders, and focused largely on the impact of changing policies and legislation during the twentieth century. In this chapter we concentrate on contemporary residential work with offenders, and draw heavily on the accounts of hostel workers in order to consider how actual policies translate into 'grassroots' work. We focus in particular on the impact of the publication *National Standards for the Supervision of Offenders in the Community* or *National Standards* as they are usually known for obvious reasons! These were first introduced in 1992 and subsequently revised in 1995, and again in 2000. We focus here on the 1995 version - the version in place at the time the research was conducted - but explore at the end of the chapter the key differences between the 2nd and 3rd editions.

National Standards: Origins and rationale

Although *National Standards* was not published until 1992, its origins can be traced back to 1984. This year represents a watershed in the recent history of the Probation Service (McLaughlin and Muncie, 1994). In this year the Home Office published its *Statement of National Objectives and Priorities*, usually abbreviated to SNOP, as part of the government's Financial Management Initiative. Officially it was described as an attempt by the Home Office to take more direct and positive action to secure improvements in local management and performance (see National Audit Office, 1989). However its critics viewed it as something altogether more fearsome, particularly once it had been published with a title very different to the rather bland one accompanying earlier versions *(The Future Direction of the Probation Service)*. SNOP has been described by Mathieson (1992, p.151) as a 'penetrating government intervention' and the beginnings of a process of tighter control to ensure each probation area had local statements in line with the Home Office national statement. For Mathieson (1992), SNOP was one consequence of the government's commitment to encouraging 'value for money' and promoting 'law and order'. On the former point, Brownlee (1998) argues that resources are now determining policy rather than the other way round. Part of SNOP's controversial nature stemmed from the fact that it aimed to encourage a degree of uniformity and consistency in order to promote accountability in a service which had previously celebrated its diversity. In addition, it prioritised the work of the Probation Service in both the provision of alternatives to custody and the preparation of social inquiry reports (now pre-sentence reports). Other duties such as prisoner throughcare and court welfare work were given a low priority. The focus of the Probation Service was thus moved away from assisting minor offenders in need of social work intervention to working with categories of offenders thought to be at risk to society. However, by attempting to move the Probation Service 'up-tariff', it moved officers away from working with client groups which they had historically served (see Brownlee, 1998). Given the contentious nature of this reform perhaps then it was of no surprise to find that a review of local statements revealed continuing diversity in responses, underpinned by differences in philosophy (Lloyd, 1986).

SNOP clearly pointed to the direction that relations between local services and central government would take in the future. The changes foreshadowed in SNOP were realised incrementally by further prescriptive policy documents published by central government which were aimed directly at Probation Service personnel. Four years later in 1988, *National Standards for Community Service Orders* were introduced which aimed to make community service orders consistently tough and demanding, thus increasing support amongst both the public and sentencers for this community penalty (Brownlee, 1998). These standards were followed by the introduction of national standards for all aspects of probation work in 1992. *National Standards* followed hot on the heels of the 1991 Criminal

36

Justice Act which aimed to reserve imprisonment for the most serious offenders and punish the bulk of offenders in the community. In practice, a policy of 'punitive bifurcation' (Cavadino and Dignan, 1997) was pursued as the 1991 Criminal Justice Act was implemented, and attempts were made to 'toughen up' community sentences. *National Standards* was part of this process in that it emphasised the role of community penalties in restricting the liberty of offenders and making real mental, and in some instances physical, demands on them (Brownlee, 1998). The introduction of *National Standards* was only one 'nail in the coffin of local autonomy and a further centralisation of policy making power' (Cavadino et al, 1999; p.104). Other examples include periodic reviews by the Audit Commission, National Audit Office and HM Inspectorate of Probation, plus the introduction of cash-limited budgets in 1992.

National Standards for the Supervision of Offenders in the Community was published jointly by the Home Office, Department of Health and Welsh Office (now National Assembly for Wales) as required standards of practice for probation services in England and Wales. The 1995 version of *National Standards* covered the following areas of probation activity:

1.   Pre-sentence reports.
2.   Probation orders.
3.   Supervision orders.
4.   Community service orders.
5.   Combination orders.
6.   Supervision before and after release from custody.
7.   The management of approved probation and bail hostels.
8.   Bail information schemes.

It is claimed that *National Standards* are relevant to a wide range of groups. The main stakeholders include victims; individual probation services (committees and probation staff); the criminal courts; offenders and the public. Further stakeholders include other criminal justice agencies and professions, for example the police and the legal profession); other public sector bodies (for example, social services and health authorities); the private sector (for example, private security companies involved in electronic monitoring) and voluntary sector agencies that the Probation Service work in partnership with (for example, those who work with substance users). As a consequence of the large number of stakeholders involved *National Standards* needs to balance a wide range of interests, and these are partially reflected in the aims of the standards.

In the opening pages, a statement of general aim is given:

> to strengthen the supervision of offenders in the community, providing punishment and a disciplined programme for offenders, building on the skill and experience of practitioners and managers.
>
> (Home Office, 1995, p.2)

The means by which these aims will be achieved is also stated (Home Office, 1995, p.2 - emphasis in original):

- by setting clear **requirements** for supervision, understood by all concerned
- by enabling service practitioners' **professional judgement** to be exercised within a framework of **accountability**
- by encouraging the adoption of **good practice** including the development of local practice guidelines (which should be in line with the requirements set by the standards)
- by ensuring that supervision is delivered **fairly, consistently** and **without improper discrimination**
- by setting a priority on the **protection of the public** from re-offending (and from fear of crime)
- by establishing the importance of considering the **effect of crime on victims**
- by ensuring the public can have confidence that supervision in the community is an **effective punishment** and a means to help offenders become responsible members of the community.

Supervising officers are required to ensure that supervision is conducted in accordance with each national standard and with regard to practice guidance issued by the local service (guidance is given on the form and content of these). The role of Chief Probation Officers is defined in more detail as being 'responsible and accountable to the employing Probation Committee for leadership of probation staff and those acting under their direction to meet the requirement of each National Standard' (Home Office, 1995, p.2). *National Standards* also addresses the following issues: accountability (to be discussed in chapter eight); equal opportunities (already discussed in chapter two), liaison with other agencies and good public relations.

There was a sound professional rationale behind the publication of *National Standards* (Worrall, 1997a). Whilst some professionals welcomed diversity, many felt that there was a need to standardise some very variable and inconsistent practices across the country and between officers; not least because of the equal opportunities issues involved. Additionally it was felt that whilst professional autonomy has many positive aspects it could also be used as a cover-up for aspects of poor probation practice.

Criticisms of *National Standards* are plentiful (Waterhouse, 2000). Some have argued that they are overly-detailed and procedural, encouraging a bureaucratic approach to practice which restricts professional discretion, risk-taking and innovation, thus creating a dependency culture. Others have suggested that they are too ambiguous, hard to measure and difficult to define. They have additionally been viewed as over long, but at the same time people have been reluctant to suggest what could be left out. The need to revise them frequently to keep pace with broader changes in criminal justice policy – there have been three editions published in the space of eight years – is laborious, time-consuming and no doubt costly. The key question overall appears to be whether the introduction of *National Standards* has routinised practice and undermined the exercise of professional judgement by providing everything you needed to know in a glossy ring-bound booklet (Worrall, 1997a). As Hughes (2001) argues, the imposition of *National Standards* on the Probation Service throughout the 1990s was indicative both of the sustained assault on the previous professional autonomy of the occupation, and of the wish to transform the Probation Service from a service chiefly concerned with client rehabilitation to that of offender control. He suggests that the publication of *National Standards* was a contribution to these toughening, centralising and de-professionalising developments. Similarly, Worrall (1997a) suggests that *National Standards* impinged on the professional autonomy of 'grassroots' probation officers far more than other recent developments, including the 1991 Criminal Justice Act. Earlier developments had the greatest impact on managers and policy-makers, but *National Standards* went beyond offering broad policy guidelines, and offered detailed instructions about the administration of orders. It covered issues such as the frequency of contact, record-keeping, rules about enforcement and the taking of breach action, and the content of supervision sessions. *National Standards* placed too much emphasis on the management of supervision rather than is content. Worrall views the introduction of *National Standards* as an attempt to make individual probation officers more accountable to management and management more accountable to government. These measures fitted nicely with the rhetoric of the Citizen's Charter but without a commitment to upholding the rights of offenders or other service users. Whether *National Standards* offers an opportunity to promote good practice or represents an attempt by government to command rather persuade, and as example of prescription and formalism (Brownlee, 1998) will now be examined with specific reference to residential work with offenders.

National Standards and the management of approved bail and probation hostels: A view from hostel workers

National Standards for the management of approved bail and probation hostels covers the following areas (Home Office, 1995; reproduced in Appendix A):

1. Purpose of approved hostels
2. Information to courts and other agencies
3. Information to prospective residents
4. Admission policy
5. Induction of residents
6. Rules of the hostel
7. Supervision and enforcement
8. Information to be recorded
9. Performance monitoring.

In this chapter we explore three of the nine areas; one, six and seven. In chapter five, we consider admissions policies within hostels and in chapter eight we discuss performance monitoring in approved hostels.

The purpose of approved hostels: Do they offer an enhanced level of supervision?

The 1995 version of *National Standards* states that:

> The purpose of approved hostels is to provide an enhanced level of supervision to enable certain bailees and offenders to remain under supervision in the community.

A precise definition of the term 'enhanced supervision' is not offered but the expectation that residents should 'go to work or attend projects, training courses or treatment[1] facilities *in the community*' (emphasis in original) is included, and it is stated that hostel staff should develop a regime (see Appendix A). In the most recent thematic inspection of approved probation and bail hostels (HM Inspectorate of Probation, 1998), enhanced supervision is operationalised and includes the following:

- High levels of contact between staff and residents as part of the ongoing, daily routine of a 24 hour supervised regime.
- Daily/weekly meetings for all residents which focused on the day-to-day operation of the hostel.
- Offence focused and needs related programmes and facilities.
- Regular key working including formal and informal supervision sessions.
- Constructive activities designed to promote socially acceptable behaviour.
- Engagement with community resources.
- Strict enforcement of hostel rules and imposed conditions.
- Use of CCTV and other security measures.[2]
- Regular liaison with appropriate statutory and voluntary organisations, including the police.

Analysis of the accounts of hostel workers reveals that whilst they were often providing an enhanced level of supervision as defined above, there were some key areas of divergence from this official stance. This was particularly marked in relation to the expectation that hostel residents should work or be engaged in education or training. It was noted in virtually all the interviews conducted with hostel staff that rarely were any residents employed or enrolled on education or training courses. It was strongly felt that the expectation within *National Standards* that residents should be involved in these activities was unrealistic.

> I'm realistic and I'm very aware as well that a lot of the people we get are quite young and they've never experienced full-time employment. For me to sit there and try to pretend to them that they should be going out to look for a job when they are more worried about when they are next going to see their family or getting sent to prisons, or where they are going to get their next lot of drugs from is

41

impractical . . . I know its part of national standards and I know that's what we are supposed to be working towards but I'm going to need quite a bit of convincing.

(Assistant manager, North Street Hostel)

Others made the point that many people they work with are in crisis situations when they arrive in approved hostels and therefore 'are not in a position to even start thinking about jobs' (Assistant manager, Victoria House). One hostel worker noted that this ideal fails to recognise the difficulties offenders face in seeking work as a result of their criminal records (see Crow, 1996). Having to provide a hostel address constitutes an additional disadvantage. Some residents did choose to develop their literacy skills, or to increase their employability by attending IT courses. Two staff members, both working in women-only hostels, felt that issues of work, education and training were often overlooked and a more proactive approach could be adopted. The deputy manager at Victoria House noted the potentially damaging assumption that women do not want to access these opportunities because they have child care responsibilities

Engaging residents in constructive activities designed to promote socially acceptable behaviour was also problematic. Residents appeared to spend a significant proportion of their day 'hanging around' the hostel. All four hostels found it difficult to organise a range of activities. Instead, hostel staff tried to encourage residents to go along to community-based activities, and this varied from area to area depending on what was available locally. Hostel staff may have had a more inclusive view of what constituted constructive activities than HM Inspectorate of Probation (1998). This is illustrated in the following comments from the manager of Carlton House.

I've come to the belief that what we need to do is put on more recreational sorts of things. The fact is that this is getting people together in sessions on hairdressing or beauty, these things make people feel better about themselves and we work on people that way. You can also mix in a bit of health awareness and some drug and alcohol stuff as well.

Thus wide-ranging and enjoyable activities can be used as a 'trojan horse' for promoting socially acceptable behaviour, as well as having value in their own right. The manager felt that this type of activity may be viewed negatively, and she needed to justify spending scarce resources on this rather than offending behaviour programmes.

National Standards also makes it clear that approved hostels should be reserved for those who require enhanced supervision and are not simply meant for accommodation. It is argued that they should provide a supportive and structured environment within which their residents could be supervised effectively. In general terms, staff in the two women-only hostels tended to emphasise the supportive aspects of supervision whilst staff in the mixed and men-only hostels emphasised the structured aspects of their hostel regimes. However, all agreed that the two elements were essential for the effective supervision of hostel residents During the fieldwork a number of examples were witnessed of how hostels may in a small number of instances serve primarily as an accommodation resource. These included providing accommodation for those who had been acquitted or received a community penalty with nowhere to move on to and providing accommodation for a vulnerable young woman who was released from custody with nowhere to live. However, in most instances hostels were offering something far greater than accommodation but opportunities on offer were not always taken up. One reason for this could be that the resident did not feel that the support on offer was needed at that particular point in time:

> Part of what we do is a containment exercise waiting for the time
> when they are ready to move on to something.
>
> (Deputy manager, Harding House)

Other hostel staff held on to the view that residents, particularly bailees, should have choices about whether to take up support on offer.

> We offer people [i.e. bailees] the opportunity to live in the
> community and the opportunity to address some of the stuff
> highlighted on their assessment, some of the reasons why they came
> here in the first place if they wish to, and I stress if they wish to.
>
> (Deputy manager, North Street Hostel)

For some residents, there is a large gap between opportunities offered and those actually taken up. *National Standards* thus provides a 'paper' account of the purpose of hostels and outlines a number of expectations for residents. In practice, these are discussed with residents as opportunities but the reality is that these are not frequently taken up. In such instances, the purpose of the approved hostel may simply amount to offering accommodation and ensuring that the requirements of the court are met. This feeling was articulated by two hostel workers:

> Primarily it's a bail place. You try and offer a lot more besides so it's not just a place to stay as directed by the courts – to offer them support and general help with anything linked to the situations they are in.
>
> (Assistant manager, Victoria House)

> The main thing we offer for the majority of residents because of their lifestyles – they are chaotic or whatever – is basically a roof over their heads, an alternative to custody. It really is as basic as that. We've talked about the different things we do but it's not always appropriate for people or they don't always take it up and it boils down to an alternative to custody.
>
> (Assistant manager, Victoria House)

The realities of providing support to residents is discussed in further detail in chapter seven around three central issues: substance use, violence within relationships and offending behaviour.

Hostel staff also emphasised key roles that approved hostels could play above and beyond those identified in *National Standards*. Many of the workers in women-only hostels believed that a women-only environment could be beneficial for female residents. Based on their working knowledge that a high percentage of female residents had been abused in childhood and/or adulthood, and that some were continuing in abusive relationships, they argued that one of the crucial roles of women-only hostels was their ability to provide what they variously termed a 'safe environment', 'a breathing space' and 'a place of respite'.

> At least 90% of the women have had traumatic experiences due to men. I think for them to have an opportunity for an all female environment can be extremely useful. It gives them an opportunity to spend time without their male companions hanging around telling them what they should be doing. I think it also shows that women can do things by themselves and that is a very positive thing.
>
> (Deputy manager, Victoria House)

It was also argued that a women-only environment offers more than a place of respite but also provides women with opportunities to make changes to their lives.

> Here because it removes all the power relations between men and women, it gives them a chance to think things through on their own and that does work. It's worked so many times for so many people.
> (Manager, Carlton House)

> It provides them with the space while they are here on their own to look at themselves, to put themselves first and sort themselves out.
> (Deputy manager, Victoria House)

In many ways staff felt that hostels for women served a similar purpose to a refuge. However, unlike a refuge male visitors were allowed to visit but their visits were restricted to certain hours of the day. In this way the privacy and safety of female residents was maintained but balanced with a consideration of the rights of residents to maintain relationships with men.

In discussing the purpose of approved hostels, staff interviewed invariably talked about their attitudes to imprisonment during the course of the interview. They varied considerably in their views but all felt that hostels had many advantages over imprisonment. Many of their accounts emphasised the positive work done in hostels which they felt could not be achieved in a prison setting. For example,

> It's a far superior option to being remanded into custody and the main reason for that is because they've got relative freedom here . . . I think we work quite positively with them on their offending behaviour and sorting things out in their life as well . . . It gives them a chance to keep in touch with their families. I don't think it's a good thing for people to be totally removed from society. Here it is halfway, well I see it as halfway. Well there are extra restrictions and they are offered extra support.
> (Assistant manager, North Street Hostel)

> I think there is a lot of positive work done in bail hostels which it would be impossible to do in custody. Especially the fact that they are still able to have contact with their families and with their children which is so important.
> (Assistant manager, Victoria House)

45

Others felt that simply keeping someone out of prison was of value *per se.* This opinion was advocated by those who were firmly wedded to the idea that imprisonment was not necessary for the vast majority of offenders. For instance,

> Hopefully if nothing else it's somewhere to stay that isn't prison while they are on bail.
>
> (Manager, North Street Hostel)

One manager did have mixed feeling about the value of hostels.

> It think it's just a second chance really. I mean they are all on the borderline of getting remanded into custody. I think on the whole that it might be better for them to go into custody which might sound strange but I have got ideas about that. I do think it gives them a chance to actually sit back and review what they want to do even if they go to prison. It gives them a second chance . . . That period can give them a chance to tie up loose ends, say goodbye to people, to make plans and that is so beneficial.
>
> (Manager, Carlton House)

When questioned further about the idea that it might be better for them to go into custody, she explained that time spent on remand in custody is taken into account if a custodial sentence is given by the courts. This is not the case for a period of time in a hostel. Thus for those who are pleading guilty to offences which will inevitably lead to a custodial sentence, it might be better for them to spent time in custody, in other words begin their sentence before it was formally given, rather than delay the inevitable.

Rules, regulation and enforcement

Strict enforcement of hostel rules and conditions is regarded as one dimension of enhanced supervision (HM Inspectorate of Probation, 1998). *National Standards* states that each hostel should have a set of rules detailing the requirements and restrictions on residents when they are on the premises, including the hostel grounds and any cluster properties.[3] It is also stipulated that the rules should be prominently displayed in the hostel and consideration be given as to whether they should be made available in appropriate minority languages. The rules should prohibit:

- Violent, threatening or disruptive language or conduct.
- Disorderly, threatening or abusive behaviour as a result of drink or drug abuse.
- The use of controlled drugs, other than on prescription and following notification to hostel staff.
- Any conduct or language that might reasonably give serious offence to hostel staff, other residents or members of the public.
- Theft or damage to the property of the hostel, staff or other residents.

The rules should also require payment of the agreed weekly charge by the resident when due, except in the circumstances when this payment may be waived.[4] A further rule is that residents must return to the hostel by a fixed time each evening, usually 11pm, unless the court orders an earlier curfew. They are required to remain in the hostel until 6am.

Analysis of the accounts of the hostel workers across all four hostels revealed a number of common themes. The first area of agreement was that serious or repeated infringements of the hostel rules constitute grounds for breach action. This is entirely compatible with *National Standards*. In some instances, residents were breached and then a decision was made to accept the resident again. No mention of this flexibility is made in *National Standards*. The second area on which hostel workers agreed was that the different hostel rules should serve different purposes. Some rules were there to protect staff, other residents and the public, for example those prohibiting disorderly, threatening or abusive behaviour. However, the enforcement of other rules might play a more educational role. For example, the use of racist language might be dealt with informally by highlighting the offensive nature of the remark.

There were also some common concerns. The principal ones surrounded the lack of consistency within hostels teams relating to rule enforcement. Typical comments included:

> I must admit that we are not very consistent about some things and I find that extremely frustrating . . . You find yourself defending other staff's decisions that are not necessarily what you would do.
>
> (Assistant manager, North Street Hostel)

> It's frustrating for us and for residents when they see inconsistencies.
>
> (Assistant manager, North Street Hostel)

It is very difficult if they are not all treated the same by everybody and they aren't.

(Night support worker, Harding House)

All four hostels had chosen to keep the number of rules to a minimum and avoided making the rules too specific. The advantages of this approach were articulated by the manager of Victoria House.

The rules allow us to breach people when we need to. They are flexible enough to ensure the women within the hostel are able to have a quiet life if they want to without feeling that everything is regulated. I think that if you have too many you are bound to get people breaking them. Having broad rules ensures that we can use them if we need to. I suppose that does mean that we are applying them when we think it is necessary rather than specifically.

Staff had considerable discretion when responding to the behaviour of residents. Whilst welcomed as providing opportunities for flexibility, it also made it difficult to ensure that residents were treated the same.

Prohibition of the use of controlled drugs was highlighted as particularly problematic. It was emphasised that it was difficult to actually know whether residents had been using illegal drugs on hostel premises.

I'm not sure how we can be expected to deal with drug use in the hostel. We obviously can't do urine tests or anything like that. You know it goes on but what can you do. We have to condone blatant drug use. You can usually spot if someone has been smoking cannabis but you can't detect the use of other drugs so easily.

(Assistant manager, Harding House)

However even if there was evidence of drug use, this would not automatically lead to a breach action because hostel staff then had to prove who was responsible.

With some drugs you can smell them but you can't pinpoint who has taken it. Unless you've seen that person take it you can't do anything about it.

(Assistant manager, Carlton House)

48

If it was clear that a particular resident had been using illegal drugs on the premises this inevitably led to breach action. This appeared to be the only response possible under the current legal framework.

> With drugs because they are illegal it is ever so difficult. What I'd like to do is say if any cannabis is found the person gets a warning but the fact that at present it is illegal means we have to breach people.
>
> (Manager, Carlton House)

> Because of the legal implications you have to be quite hard on drugs. If they are found with drugs in their room they are breached.
>
> (Deputy manager, North Street Hostel)

Victoria House had a high concentration of women residents who were problem drug users, often injecting heroin and sometimes using crack cocaine. Harm reduction policies had evolved to minimise the risk presented from accommodating drugs users, especially injecting users. These policies were not entirely unproblematic:

> We provide sharps boxes. It's quite strange. You are saying to people that you are not allowed to use in the hostel but we know if someone has a drug problem the chances are that they will so we provide sharps boxes.
>
> (Assistant manager, Victoria House)

> We are saying that you aren't allowed drugs in the hostel but the fact is that we recognise that you do by providing sharps boxes. There are mixed messages there.
>
> (Assistant manager, Victoria House).

> Sharps boxes do give mixed messages and its not something that we have introduced lightly . . . It's safer for us . . . just because I say you can't use in the hostel won't make the problem go away.
>
> (Manager, Victoria House)

The research discussed in this text predates the Wintercomfort case. This involved the prosecution in 1999 of Ruth Wyner, Director of Wintercomfort and John Brock, the charity's day centre manager. They were given custodial sentences for knowingly permitting the use of heroin on the premises because some of the people they were helping were secretly exchanging drugs on the premises. Their sentences were later reduced on appeal. Coupled with the proposed amendment to Section 8 of the Misuse of Drugs Act 1971 which obliges managers to stop the use of *all* controlled drugs, this issue is likely to be a pressing one for hostel managers. In 1998 a probation circular entitled *Guidance on Working with Drug Misusers in Approved Probation and Bail Hostels* was issued. This may need revision. In the meantime, hostel managers could also turn to guidance principally aimed at managers of hostels for the homeless published by Drugscope (Britton and Pamneja, 2001)

The 1995 and 2000 versions: A comparison

The 2000 version no longer applies to the supervision of offenders under 18. A national Youth Justice Board was established in October 1998 to monitor the operation of the youth justice system, promote good practice and advise the Home Secretary on the operation of the youth justice system and the setting of national standards. This was introduced as part of the radical changes to operation of the youth justice system under New Labour, and was created by the 1998 Crime and Disorder Act. The rationale behind the creation of the board was to develop a national focus for driving the far-reaching reforms forward. At a local level multi-agency youth offending teams were introduced to provide, co-ordinate and run local youth justice systems in accordance with national standards and guidelines.

There are further differences between the versions of *National Standards* published in 1995 and 2000. Some of these differences reflect broader changes in criminal justice and social policy such as the emphasis on effective practice (see chapter eight); a greater commitment to assessing and managing risk (see chapter five) and a renewed interest in partnership working. However the publication also provides a new direction for the Probation Service. The quote by Paul Boateng, the Minister for Prisons and Probation, on the opening page gives some indication as to what lies inside: 'WE ARE A LAW ENFORCEMENT AGENCY. It's what we are. It's what we do' (Emphasis in original).

One of the most significant departures from the 1995 version of *National Standards* is the requirement that breach proceedings should follow after a single statutory warning. This is coupled with a requirement under the Criminal Justice and Court Services Act 2000 to impose a prison sentence on those who are breached. Hedderman and Hough (2000) see no particular problem with the move to a single warning, however they argue that the introduction of a near mandatory prison sentence is bad law because it offends against principles of proportionality, is impractical and represents poor value for money. In a similar vein Ellis (2000) argues that current enforcement policy and practices need a more balanced evidence-led approach that will increase sentencer and public confidence without resorting to making tough sounding, but ultimately futile, promises.

The changing face of approved hostels – according to National Standards *(2000)*

In the 2000 version (reproduced in Appendix B), the purpose of approved hostels is clarified and there is a more explicit commitment to public protection.

> The purpose of approved hostels is to provide an enhanced level of residential supervision with the aim of protecting the public by reducing the likelihood of offending. Approved hostels are for bailees, probationers, and post-custody licencees, where their risk of serious harm to the public or other likelihood of reoffending means that no other form of accommodation in the community would be suitable.

One of the major changes in the 2000 *National Standards* is the operationalisation of what is meant by an enhanced level of supervision. It is now stated that approved hostels enhance supervision in that they:

- impose a supervised nighttime curfew which can be extended to other times of the day (e.g. as required by a court order or licence condition);
- provide 24 hour staff oversight;
- undertake ongoing assessment of attitudes and behaviour;
- require compliance with the clearly stated house rules which are rigorously enforced;
- provide a programme of regular supervision, support and daily monitoring that tackles offending behaviour and reduce risks.

This is likely to be a response to the 1998 HM Inspectorate of Probation report on approved hostels which argued that:

a revised national statement about the purpose of hostels in the future is needed which specifies what an enhanced level of supervision must include.

(HM Inspectorate of Probation, 1998, p.57)

Some of the change introduced were simply keeping pace with wider changes in criminal justice policy. A section is now included on arrangements for electronic monitoring. Home Detention Curfews, introduced in the 1998 Crime and Disorder Act, permit short-term prisoners (with sentences of less than four years) to be released into the community up to two months prior to their normal release date. In the first sixteen months of the scheme, over 21,000 prisoners were released (Dodgson et al, 2001) and some of these were accommodated in approved hostels. A further group of residents may have had electronic monitoring imposed as a condition of a parole licence.

Other changes had been made to keep pace with changes which had already been made to hostel working practices. For instance it is now stated that local house rules should prohibit the use of alcohol and solvents on hostel premises. Recognising the links between alcohol and crime, and the dangers of solvent use, many hostels already disallowed the use of these substances. In the four hostels, only one (Victoria House) allowed alcohol to be drunk in the hostel, and then only in the resident's room rather than the communal resident's lounge. This hostel was managed by a voluntary organisation and its policy was out of line with the local probation service which had made all other hostels in the area 'dry'. At the time of the research, staff at Victoria House felt under pressure to change their policy.

There are also some examples of changes where the emphasis has shifted from offering guidance to being rather prescriptive. For instance, it is now clearly stated that admissions will be based on risk assessment procedure and that these procedures will involved the relevant elements of OASys, a risk assessment tool. Indeed the whole emphasis of this section is on risk assessment and management.

A further significant change is that content of supervision is actually operationalised in the 2000 version. It is now stated that supervision should include the following:

- address and reduce offending behaviour;
- challenge offenders to accept responsibility for the crimes committed and their consequences;
- contribute to the protection of the public;

52

- motivate and assist residents towards a greater sense of personal responsibility and discipline;
- aid reintegration of offenders as law-abiding members of the community.

Whilst this may be welcomed as a move towards standardisation of variable practices, others may feel that it represents further impingement upon professional autonomy.

Two areas of change are likely to be of concern to at least some of the hostel workers interviewed for this study. Firstly, the distinction between different resident groups, that is those of probation, those on bail and those under post-release supervision is no longer made. It may be that such distinctions continue to operate in practice. Secondly, amendments have been made to enforcement practices in approved hostels. The distinction between serious and repeated, as opposed to minor infringements continues, being dealt with by immediate breach action and informal warnings respectively. However, the system of two formal warnings for failure to return by the required time without an acceptable excuse has been reduced to one. Given the nature of the client group, strict enforcement of this could result in increased breaches from approved hostels.

Concluding comments

There is no doubt that the introduction of *National Standards* has had a much greater impact than any previous guidance or policy initiative. Whether or not they have been adhered to in the round, they are perceived as highly significant by managers and practitioners, not least because inspections monitor adherence to, and the achievement of, the standards. For those working in hostels, the main concern was that *National Standards* included too many idealistic aspirations and failed to appreciate the realities of working with a client group experiencing multiple, complex problems. Frequently the prescriptions within *National Standards* were interpreted liberally to fit with staff expectations of the purpose of approved hostels. This is unlikely to be what the Home Office intended but it does allow potentially competing views on the role of approved hostels to be reconciled.

Waterhouse (2000) suggests that future national standards should have the following attributes: reflect the interest of a wide range of stakeholders;

support principles of effective practice identified through research and other evaluative activity; address key elements of service delivery including objectives, inputs, processes, outputs and outcomes; and be developed collaboratively. He argues that on this basis it should be possible to develop standards by identifying desired objectives and outcomes, and by setting standards for the inputs, processes and outputs which support their achievement. Standards should not deal in detail with legislation, procedures or working methods, which, where necessary, can be the subject of related guidance or annexed to the standards. He argues that in part the 2000 version of *National Standards* fulfil these attributes. However, he raises two concerns. First, he raises the question about whether a very rigid approach to enforcement can be reconciled with the positive exercise of discretion in pursuit of effective practice, and notes that probation officers now have considerably less discretion that their colleagues working in other parts of the criminal justice system. Second, he questions whether sufficient emphasis has been given to the active promotion of the social inclusion of offenders as part of any plans to address problems related to their offending and to reintegrate them into society. His concerns are likely to be echoed by those engaged in residential work with offenders.

Notes

1.   The term 'treatment' is not defined but is assumed to mean help for drug or alcohol dependency, or rehabilitation for physical and mental health problems.

2.   The use of security measures in the three hostels which accommodated women is discussed in Wincup, E. (2001a) 'Managing Security in Semi-Penal Institutions for Women', *Security Journal*, vol. 4, pp.41-51.

3.   This term refers to properties which are part of the hostel but not attached to it. They could include properties in the hostel grounds or flats and houses located close by. They are managed by hostel staff but residents are do not receive the same degree of supervision as other residents. They are used in particular for long-term bailees and those on probation, subject to a risk assessment.

4.   Residents are required to contribute some of their benefits or wages towards the payment of the weekly charge. Exceptions may be made in some cases, e.g. for foreign nationals who are not entitled to benefits or permitted to work.

4 Falling in at the Deep End: Becoming a Hostel Worker

I suppose I did feel like I'd fallen in at the deep end when I actually
started but I was OK as I went along.

(Assistant manager, North Street Hostel)

If any job in the Probation Service has a tendency to throw people in
the deep end then it is this one [i.e. being a hostel worker]!

(Osler, 1995, p.44)

Working with offenders in residential settings is perhaps more challenging
than other forms of probation work. Hostels assemble individuals with
multiple and complex problems who are compelled to live together by the
courts in conditions which are sometimes far from ideal. Staff work long
shifts with few breaks, sometimes being required to sleep in the hostel and
are constantly working face-to-face with their clients. This can be
particularly daunting for new workers. This chapter draws on the
experiences of workers new to residential work with offenders, and
recollections of established staff of their early days, and offers sociological
analyses of the process of becoming a residential worker.

Hostel workers: Career paths and aspirations

The residential workers interviewed brought with them a wealth of relevant
experience acquired in a range of settings. Fourteen of the hostel staff
interviewed (including the four probation officers) had experience of
working with offenders either in the criminal justice system as police
officers, probation officers or assistants, bail information officers, relief
hostel workers and probation volunteers or through voluntary agencies
such as NACRO. Half the sample had experience of working in residential
settings with different client groups and/or working in social care settings,
particularly with young people. The probation officers working within the
hostels as deputy managers and managers were less likely to have
experience of residential care and prior to working in the hostel had, in

most cases, been working in field teams. This parallels the findings of the Home Office Inspection of Approved Probation and Bail Hostels (1993). The subsequent one published in 1998, reported that many assistant managers believed their skills and experience were not recognised by their colleagues working outside the service. Similarly, the assistant managers and night support workers who participated in this study felt that working with offenders in residential settings is one of the most difficult tasks undertaken by the Probation Service but is often regarded as low status work and as an adjunct to mainstream probation work. Typical comments included:

> We're very much on a limb as regards the service even though we are supposedly part of the Probation Service. We are like a sidings in a way.
>
> (Assistant manager, Harding House)

> I think we are a bit distanced, It would be nice to know a bit more about what is going on.
>
> (Assistant manager, Harding House)

We will return to this point later in the chapter because their feelings of isolation have consequent implications for the shaping of their professional identities.

It is a commonly held view that being an assistant manager or night support worker in a hostel is a 'stepping stone' for those who wishing to enter probation training. This can result in a high turnover staff as people stay in hostels for a year or so in order to gain the minimum required experience (Worrall, 1997a). The Probation Service routinely collects 'wastage' statistics on staff leaving, excluding death, retirement and transfer. In 1995, the figure was 11 percent. However it should be noted that the percentage of men leaving was twice as high as for women, and women comprise over half the staff in hostels (Home Office, 1997).

The assistant managers and night support workers interviewed had spent an average of two years five months working in their current hostel. Their length of service ranged from five months to eight years. Some had also worked as a relief worker in the same hostel prior to commencing full-time employment. There was little evidence that individuals had made conscious decisions to become an assistant manager or night support worker as a means of securing access to probation training. Only two of the workers, both based at Harding House, had an aspiration to become qualified probation officers. In one case, the desire to train as a probation officer had arisen as a consequence of enjoying work within the hostel rather than being their intention from the outset. For one assistant manager, working in the hostel had actually put her off becoming a probation officer.

> I did think I wanted to be a probation officer for a while but of course the training has changed and that sort of put me off a little bit. The more I found out about the Probation Service and its work with offenders, the more I found out it was so restrictive. There isn't really a lot on offer for offenders in terms of rehabilitation. It's just very negative. So now I don't really want to be a probation officer. It's just too bureaucratic really with too much interference from government.
>
> (Assistant manager, North Street Hostel)

Two other assistant managers talked about their desire to undergo social work training (Diploma in Social Work) although their plans were rather vague and in the short-term they planned to continue with residential work.

> I might do social work training but not probation. I don't know.
>
> (Assistant manager, Victoria House)

> I want to do a DipSW but I'm not sure of the timescale . . . It is in my mind.
>
> (Assistant manager, Victoria House)

The remaining members of staff saw their work as a career in itself. For example, one worker commented:

> It's not a means to an end for me [i.e. a way of accessing probation training]. I'm doing this now because that's what I want to do at the moment.
>
> (Assistant manager, North Street Hostel)

The difficulty for these members of staff is that few opportunities for career development are available. The requirement to have a probation qualification to be appointed to the post of deputy manager or manager creates a barrier to subsequent promotion.

57

What all the hostel workers brought to their work was a wealth of relevant experience, albeit acquired in very different settings. Assistant managers and night support workers are often described as unqualified staff but they often bring a width and depth of experience from other work. Consequently, hostel staff have a number of transferable skills which can be adapted and developed. This can be achieved through training which relates to the demands of the post. However, as the following discussion will illustrate training was not always perceived as adequate and despite their wealth of relevant experience, the first few months working in hostel for offenders were anxious times.

Early days

At the time the interviews took place, two assistant managers had been in post for less than six months and a further three (one deputy manager, two assistant mangers) had less than one year's experience of residential work with offenders. Exploring their experiences provides a great insight into the experiences of becoming a hostel worker.

> I suppose I did feel like I'd fallen in at the deep end when I actually started but I was OK as I went along.
>
> (Assistant manager, North Street Hostel)

The comment above by a member of staff who had only been working in a bail and probation hostel for a few months suggests that becoming a hostel worker is a daunting process. In her own words, she described the ways in which her enthusiasm for the job and her belief that she could do it were mixed with unnerving feelings because of the expectation that she begin to do it without any initial training.

All the staff interviewed had received some training during the period they had been working in hostels. The 1993 HM Inspectorate of Probation thematic review of approved hostels argued for:

> core training for all hostel staff at all levels, certain key elements of which need to be delivered before or soon after the postholder takes up an appointment.
>
> (HM Inspectorate of Probation, 1993, p.66)

Training courses on specific issues such as basic counselling, the criminal justice system, supporting drug and alcohol users and handling violence and aggression provided assistant managers and night support workers with an overview of appropriate approaches. In three of the four areas, dedicated courses were also offered to managers and deputy managers. Training opportunities were not always provided to workers at the outset, and access to training varied considerably between the four probation areas. This squares with the finding of the HM Inspectorate of Probation (1998) thematic review. The problem appeared to be a lack of a systematic approach to organising training rather than a insufficient resources or a lack of suitable courses. At North Street Hostel, attempts were being made to develop a training strategy to replace the ad hoc approach. Many of the staff were new and therefore part of the approach was to consider team training.

Staff could identify gaps in their knowledge that they required training to address but it would be wrong to give the impression that all the staff were demanding additional training. Some were quite negative about training, for example:

> I don't find training courses very valuable. You learn more from your colleagues.
>
> (Deputy manager, Harding House)

> You always learn more from the people you work with, people who have been here for a bit. There is a lot of shadowing when you first start . . . You learn a lot more through that than through training courses.
>
> (Assistant manager, Harding House)

The hostel workers quoted above may had experienced poor quality or inappropriate training in the past which may account for their negative views. It is concerning that training is perceived in this way. Others did not reject the value of training courses but argued that the application of these ideas and talking to colleagues was regarded as the main learning experience.

> They [training courses] are useful but not as useful as doing it.
>
> (Deputy manager, Carlton House)

> There were a lot of courses available and I was encouraged to partake. They were useful but basically I suppose I think the thing about residential work . . . is that's something you can either do or can't do at all. You find that out by doing the job.
>
> (Assistant manager, Harding House)

It was argued that in many ways much of the work relied upon the utilisation of personal resources which could only be developed through experiences within and outside the hostel rather than through training. Within their work there was considerable scope for the exercise of individual discretion and autonomy. However, new workers often lack the confidence to rely on their own instincts and make choices about how to proceed. In their accounts, staff discussed how their everyday work was often something they were unprepared for and felt they might have benefited from further training. For instance, one worker at Victoria House, only a few months into her work there, found herself dealing with a violent situation. Without training on how to deal with it, she locked herself in the office and called the police. She discovered later that this was seen as the 'right' thing to do, but at that time she was following her instincts rather than implementing procedures she was trained to follow. In a similar way, a new member of staff at North Street Hostel found herself relying on her skills as an individual rather than as a trained worker.

> The thought of taking groups I found absolutely scary . . . It was seen as part of the job and I just had to bluff my way though it.

The first few months inevitably lead to difficulties and anxieties which others described. Unlike other professions such as law, education and medicine, new hostel workers do not experience formalised training and therefore are unlikely to have other novices for support. Instead, they rely upon the experience and support of other workers in the team to establish their professional identities and negotiate conflicting pressures.

The occupational socialisation of hostel workers

Wright and Davies (1989, p.45) argue that the process of becoming a probation officer involves 'cultural absorption into a framework of role and function, professional identity and agency context'. This is comparable to hostel work. At the same time as individuals need to

60

establish their role and function as hostel workers, they also need to establish a professional identity and locate their work within a broader context. For probation officers, training can be a key focus of occupational socialisation. Studies of other professions have also indicated the importance of the training process in terms of occupational socialisation (Atkinson, 1981; Becker et al, 1961; Coffey, 1994). However, as discussed earlier in this chapter, for hostel work there is no centralised and standardised training rather individuals are trained in-house or through training courses run by the individual probation areas and voluntary agencies such as NACRO. Additionally, staff within hostels often feel they are at the margins of probation work. This results in the key reference group for the worker being the hostel, or more specifically the staff team within the hostel. A similar point is made by Pithouse (1987, p.7) who argued of child care workers:

> as lower participants in a larger organisation they do not look to other groups within and without the organisation as a source of reference or positive alignment. Instead . . . they secure a sense of identity and validation from their immediate colleagues in the Office setting.

From the above discussion and workers' reflections on becoming a hostel worker, an interactionist theoretical perspective on the process of socialisation appears to be the most appropriate way to explain how individuals become hostel workers. Traditionally, this perspective has been applied to professional training (Atkinson, 1983). Crucially, it focuses on day-to-day aspects of practice and ways of surviving as newcomers learn the ropes (Miller, 1970). However, as Atkinson and Delamont (1985, 1990) have argued, an important deficiency of work carried out in the interactionist tradition is that issues of power, control and knowledge are glossed over. Becoming a hostel worker involves learning a particular claim to knowledge. Jamous and Peloille (1970) suggest that occupational knowledge comprises two dimensions: technicity and indeterminacy. Technicity refers to the explicit, rule governed and codified aspects of the job. For hostel workers, this may be the application of *National Standards* or the hostel rules. However, there is some overlap here with indeterminacy, the implicit, unexamined ways of being a member of an occupational group. This relates to personal knowledge, experience and judgement. Hence, even in situations where a rule has been broken and technical knowledge is applied, flexibility and discretion are important aspects. Referring to themselves as generalists rather than specialists, hostel workers felt they had few claims to expert, technical knowledge. Knowledge is learned largely through day-to-day practice rather than through training. This has implications in terms of power and control. Acting as the 'stepping stone' in an ongoing process of change, hostel workers are largely dependent upon the actions of others to achieve their aspirations in terms of helping residents to change their lives (see chapter eight).

Establishing a professional identity

Examining how hostel workers establish a professional identity requires consideration of the role of hostels and the teams who work within them in shaping and moulding individuals who are simultaneously creating their own professional identities, drawing on their own unique experiences. Negotiating a professional identity takes places in the context of renegotiating of their personal identities. The relationship between a person's sense of who they are and paid work had been a concern, at least implicitly, of sociologists studying work throughout the twentieth century (du Gay 1996). More recently, there has been a recognition of how identities shaped by gender and ethnicity impact upon work identity in general texts (Rees, 1992; Watson, 1995) and discussion of the lived realities of patriarchal relations in the workplace (Cavendish, 1982; Pollert, 1981; Westwood, 1984). This was articulated by some of hostel workers, particularly those at North Street Hostel who had been involved in a gender awareness day. Although the event did not lead to the formulation of policies which could be translated into practice, it was seen as beneficial.

> It was more of a sound off but it was good to talk about what it meant to be a female worker and in my case a black worker. The Probation Service is very hierarchical and what came out of that is that there are different stories depending on where you are in the service.
>
> (Assistant manager, North Street Hostel)

Structural factors such as gender and race constitute an important aspect of shaping a professional identity. As we explored in chapter two, gender and racial inequalities in wider society are reflected within the Probation Service.

Professional identities are also formed through interaction and communication. Summarising the work of Mead, du Gay (1996, p.30) suggests:

> The construction of identity occurs in social organisation that arises from the mutual adaptation of conduct, or adaptation that is situated in current activity and which takes place through the medium of communication. It is in this communication, particularly through language, that individuals become self-reflexive and gain control over their responses during social activity. The values and morals of the generalised group also enter the consciousness through language and plays a significant role in the control of behaviour, taken as necessary for both social order and a harmonious existence.

This highlights some crucial issues relevant to the experience of hostel workers, although it neglects issues of race and gender. It emphasises the importance of language to communicate shared meanings which make sense of hostel work. Through interaction with others, a professional identity can be developed. Reflected within the use of language is a commitment to the general values of the group or team, an internalisation of attitudes. In this way, the team approach is strengthened and social order within the hostel is maintained.

Becoming a hostel worker involves becoming a member of a team. This was particularly relevant at Victoria House where the concept of the team was continually highlights in staff accounts. Typical comments included 'I see myself very much part of a staff team', 'we work as a team' and 'if you didn't have a sense of teamwork I don't think the hostels would work'. This may reflect the length of time the staff had worked together in comparison with other hostels such as North Street Hostel where the majority of staff were relatively new. The 'term' team was used loosely in their accounts, and may have been utilised in several different ways. In most cases it appeared to be used to described a group of people working together closely in a cohesive group rather than to refer to an identifiable administrative work unit. There have numerous attempts to classify teams, and one of the more useful attempts is by Brown and Bourne (1996). They suggest that teams differ in terms of the degree of interdependence of team members and in terms of power differentials between team members.

Teams within approved hostels can be defined as integrated teams, in the sense that all team members are working together on a common task in such a way that the effectiveness of each team member is dependent on that of their colleagues. Such teams can also be described as deputised which refers to a structure in which members are differentiated by roles (although most are of equal status) but all are directly accountable to the hostel manager. All managers were regarded as team players but at Harding House the manager was particularly praised for balancing his managerial responsibilities with occupying a 'hands on' role.

Team work within residential work has traditionally been seen as an appropriate method of working. The Central Council for Education and Training in Social Work (CCETSW) published a discussion document in 1973 which argued that teamwork was essential,

> To create a living environment to enhance the functioning of individual residents in the context of their total environment
>
> (CCETSW, 1973, p.15)

This view is supported by Douglas (1984, p. vii) who suggests,

> In a very direct sense, residential work is team work. The methods of creating an environment in which care, learning and change can take place is wholly dependent for success upon the professional staff working in a clear and accepted pattern. This often requires suspending differences of outlook and approach in order to present a united effort.

Similarly, the HM Inspectorate of Probation Thematic Review (1998) states that hostels could not operate without a high level of collaboration between all grades of staff. Team training had been offered at Victoria House and North Street Hostel, in the latter through a Home Office video inviting participants to consider how they work as a team within the hostel. This involves consideration of a number of roles team work could fulfil.

Within hostels decisions are often made as a team. Sometimes this is achieved informally through consultation with another member of staff on issues such as whether to accept a referral. At other times, decisions may involved the entire team.

Staff meetings are very much based around the evidence of working with women so we work as a team . . . It's about a team working with residents.

(Deputy manager, Victoria House)

To illustrate:

What we might do in a fight between residents is return them both to court. If we know one has been victimised and bullied for days and weeks, and had to retaliate through violence to protect herself, we might say to the court that we are willing to take her back. It's discussed amongst the staff team.

(Assistant manager, Victoria House)

Inevitably some decisions are made by staff members individually. One aspect of team work is to respect decisions made by individual workers.

If I breached a woman because I was scared I'd be supported even if other people would have done it differently.

(Assistant manager, Victoria House).

In this way the team is able to provide support for all its members and also accords individuals some degree of professional autonomy.

The hostel workers' accounts of team work relate to two functions stressed by Payne and Scott (1982): the instrumental function (getting the work done) and the expressive function (offering support to the worker). These two roles are closely related, and as Payne and Scott argue need to be balanced to provide a task-oriented environment which meets clients needs while at the same time offering support and stimulation to workers. A team approach does not require all individuals within it to agree all the time, although consensus on fundamental issues such as the role of the hostel and a commitment to equal opportunities is required. Debate can be conducive to the formulation of policy and modes of working. However compromises must be reached. Through working as a team, potential difficulties and tensions in hostel work can be discussed and ways to alleviate them found. In three of the hostels the team approach did not appear to produce tensions although staff may have wished to present a particularly harmonious image of team work. Pithouse (1994) makes similar points about his study of child care professionals. He argues that workers learn colleagueship based on an ethos of mutual support and

65

harmony, and learn that the team should act as a 'happy family'. In this way the dilemmas of practice are managed. However at Harding House the accounts of some workers shattered this harmonious image. For instance, one worker commented:

> I suppose different people have different personalities don't they which can be difficult . . . Not everyone thinks the way I do.
>
> (Night support worker, Harding House)

The differences appeared to relate to difference in attitudes regarding appropriate ways of working with residents. There was divide between those who emphasised support and flexibility (viewed by their critics as soft) and those favouring structure and rigidity (viewed by their critics as being harsh).

Occupational discourse

From the referral stage onwards, staff begin to build up a picture of the lifestyles of individual residents filtered through a referring agent, usually a probation officer. This is supplemented by the opportunities of individual residents, once they arrive at the hostel, to add their own voice at induction, through keyworking sessions and through informal conversations. Staff respond to the stories of the lived realities of unique individuals by developing frameworks which Schutz refers to as 'scheme of interpretation' (Schutz, 1967, p.86), in order to organise and make sense of practical experience. Meaning is constructed out of an individual member of staff's stream of experience, and meanings arise from the world of daily experience, as lived by the different individuals who try to make sense of it. In this way, they construct ideal-types of how the world operates. The typical resident - 'a person in crisis'- is therefore a socially constructed category representing residents with a particular type of experience and facing multiple, complex problems.

Loseke's (1992, p.165) study of a battered woman's shelter reached similar conclusions.

> Out of the buzzing confusion, heterogeneity, and complexity of lived realities, a type of experience and a type of person is produced and reproduced.

66

The sharing of stories about residents in everyday practice, formal meetings and supervision creates an occupational discourse allowing hostel workers to give meaning to their experience of working with residents. These processes also render their occupational practices visible to colleagues (see also Pithouse, 1987 for similar occupational narratives in social work teams). Sometimes these stories are disseminated beyond the boundaries of the agency to other professionals which Bull and Shaw (1992) emphasise is a central aspect of social work, and similarly hostel work. External agencies may include probation officers, workers in other hostels, drug and alcohol counsellors and court officials. The importance of sharing experiences is suggested by Pithouse and Atkinson (1988, p.185).

> Through narrative formats, tellers produce 'accounts' of their troubles, inviting sympathetic response, formulating blame and excuse. They render them dramatic, humorous or sentimental. Stories 'gain in the telling' not simply in the sense that we are prone to exaggerate and dramatise, but also in the sense that without 'the telling' events and experiences of work and domestic life would lose their meaning.

Moreover, the discussions of experiences of offenders serves as an essential element of the occupational socialisation of new workers, unqualified in terms of probation training. As discussed earlier in this chapter, their training programme consists primarily of hands-on tuition. New workers become aware at an early stage that although they experience relative autonomy when conducting their work, there are constraints which structure their accounts in a way that Schutz does not acknowledge. Notably these included pressure to be part of a team with shared goals, and pressure to use appropriate language in the 'telling', in particular probation 'jargon' and 'politically correct' terminology. Accounts contribute to occupational discourse but the same accounts are filtered through notions of occupational rhetoric.

The telling of accounts is therefore a central aspect of residential work. As Loseke (1992) observes, the development of collective representations which form occupational discourse: the 'battered woman' or the 'person in crisis' - is an ongoing social process refined through evaluating the work done to support residents and listening to stories of new residents.

Collective representations are therefore subject to change but tend to be relatively enduring both across hostels and perhaps across time. Lipsky (1980, p.59), too, refers to the way in which street-level bureaucrats, which residential workers can be considered an example of, are involved in the social process of constructing the client. He argues that unique individuals:

> are transformed into clients, identifiably located into a very small number of categories, treated as of, and treating themselves as if, they fit standardised definition of units consigned to specific bureaucratic slots.

Whilst this identifies an important dimension of hostel work, the processing of residents, it does not accurately describe the process. Rather than developing a number of categories, the typical resident is constructed - 'a person in crisis' and other residents are judged according to this benchmark. A continuum is therefore developed from 'crisis' to 'control' and residents are placed on it. The shared goal amongst staff was for residents to develop ways of taking control over their lives thus moving along the continuum. This basic goal was collectively held although notions of what constituted being 'in crisis' and being 'in control' may vary as could beliefs about the actions required for resident to move along the continuum. Residents often defined themselves in a similar way. When their future hopes were discussed, phrases like 'sorting myself out', 'settling down' and 'moving on' were frequently used.

The continuum for crisis to control is part of lay theory of why individuals offend and the approach required to challenge their offending and help them lead a law abiding life. The development of lay theories by social work and criminal justice professionals have been noted by other researchers. For example, Pithouse and Atkinson (1988, p.197) argue that social workers:

> socially organise their world through a common-sense theory that emerges from experience and maps out identities and relationships of a complex world of work.

Indeed, there is a growing body of literature on lay theories cross-cutting the social science disciplines of social psychology (Antaki, 1988; Furnham, 1988; Harre and Secord, 1972) and sociology (Pollner, 1987; Rock, 1979). Furnham elucidates some of the characteristics of lay theories, judging

68

them against academic theories which he implies are superior. He argues that they tend to be implicit, based on tacit assumptions, ambiguous, incoherent and inconsistent. These were all features of the hostel workers' accounts. Often they confused correlation and causation. For example, hostel staff at Victoria House would argue on the basis that many women in the hostel had been abused during childhood that child abuse was a cause of crime in later life. Cases would be cited of women whose experiences supported their theories in order to verify them rather than providing counter examples to refute their theories. Interestingly, their lay theories differed from Furnham's suggestion in one aspect in that they stressed structural explanations for offending rather that internal or individualistic factors. In this way, they were similarities with contemporary criminological theories which have shifted the debate in relation to crime from an emphasis on individual weakness and pathology to a focus on structural explanations. However, as Rock (1979, p.78) argues the distinction between lay and academic theories is not clear cut. He suggests that:

> Ideas of anomie, differential association, relative deprivation, functional deprivation, functional independence, conflict and labelling theory may all be found in folk wisdom, early tracts and conventional explanations. They represent parts of the common stock of everyday analysis.

Developing the continuum for crisis to control justifies the existence of approved hostels as a provider of a supportive and structured environment. It squares with the goal of the hostel worker to provide more than accommodation and an alternative to custody. Moreover, it impacts on the ways in which they respond to residents, acts an essential element of the occupational socialisation of new hostel workers and serves to create their professional identity.

Concluding comments

The research discussed in this chapter has highlighted examples of good practice. Most significantly it has identified measures taken to ensure that hostel workers are gradually eased into their work. For example, initially hostel workers are not given residents to 'key work' and then are only given small numbers of residents to work with. This parallels the tendency to give new probation officers protected caseloads (Wright and Davies, 1985). Becoming a keyworker can therefore be seen as a 'status passage' (Bucher and Stelling, 1977, p.25) when it is felt that individuals had sufficiently adjusted to everyday work around the hostel.

In many ways the concerns of new hostel workers continue throughout their work in hostels. The unpredictable nature of hostel work requires hostel workers to continually adapt to residents, new difficulties and new situations. To illustrate, what workers at Victoria House were struggling with at the time the research was conducted was to reconcile the work they had done with female survivors of abuse over the years with a realisation that an increasing number of women (although a tiny proportion of referrals) were being charged with abuse against children. Further attention needs to be given to training. These need not follow the traditional model of attendance at external courses but could involve external trainers coming in to hostels to run sessions for the team as a whole. Other residential workers could offer such training and this would provide one avenue for career development. Other possibilities might include secondment schemes whereby residential workers occupy other roles within their local probation services. Applying for probation training might be encouraged but this needs to be carefully managed to avoid problems of staff retention and frequent changes in the make up of staff teams within individual hostels.

Feelings of marginalisation amongst hostel workers should be a pressing issue for the Probation Service to address. To avoid feelings of isolation greater attention could be given to promoting links between field and residential workers. Residential workers often have little contact with other residential workers and this could be facilitated within and between local services. The fact that I was frequently asked during the course of the research what other hostels do is testimony to this!

5   Vulnerable Workers: Managing Risk and Danger

> Unlike prisons, approved probation and bail hostels are not secure establishments. Residents are neither required nor is it desirable that they should spend twenty four hours per day in the hostel. Attention to minimising the risk posed by one resident to another and residents to staff and to the public at large is, therefore, crucial.
>
> (HM Inspectorate of Probation, 1993, p.51)

Introduction

In recent years, increasing research attention has been paid to the issue of violence at work. It has been recognised that workplace violence does occur, that it can result in psychological trauma, and that interventions need to be in place to facilitate employees' responses to, and recovery from, violent events (Flannery, 1996). Indeed there is now a growing body of evidence that work-related violence is a significant occupational hazard for a wide range of occupational groups, and it has been suggested that both the frequency and severity of work-related violence are increasing (Leather et al, 1990). The 1998 British Crime Survey estimated that there were just over 1.2 million incidents of violence at work in England and Wales in 1997, comprising 523,000 physical assaults and 703,000 threats and involving 649,000 workers (Budd, 1999). Research has also highlighted that whilst violence can potentially occur in many occupational settings, particular groups are most at risk (Poyner and Warne, 1986; Budd, 1999). Those most at risk included police and probation officers and social workers; similar professions to hostel work. One explanation for this is offered by Hearden (1988). He argues that the majority of violent incidents occur when the victim is providing (or not as the case may be) a service, and the aggressor is in the role of client or customer for that service. Hostel workers clearly fit into this category. The 1998 British Crime Survey also found that many incidents occurs after 6pm (Budd, 1999). Hostel workers again fall into this high risk category because their work involves evening and night shifts.

71

Despite the potential for violence to occur within hostels as a consequence of the nature of the client group accommodated, statistics suggest that it is surprisingly rare. Between January and June 1997, of the 107 serious incidents which were reported to the Home Office, only five involved an approved hostel resident (HM Inspectorate of Probation, 1998). These figures are inevitably an underestimate and do not capture the 'dark figure' of unreported serious incidents, minor incidents and threats of violence. Nonetheless they are in some way indicative of the success of hostel workers in minimising risk. In recent years, much has been done within hostels to make them a safe place in which to live. The introduction of double cover at all times is one of the most significant changes. These reforms have taken place against a backdrop of greater attention to assessing and managing risk in relation to those who offend.

This chapter explores hostel workers' accounts of risk, danger and vulnerability, and considers their attempts to assess and manage risk as individuals and as a team. It highlights the particular dilemmas faced by hostel staff in assessing and managing risk. This will be illustrated through a discussion of two particular aspects of risk assessment and risk management in hostels: the selection of appropriate residents and the management of 'trouble'. Whilst recognising the apparently rare occurrence of violence in hostels and the achievements to date in terms of risk assessment and management, the chapter provides some suggestions for ways in which strategies to ensure the safety of hostel workers, as well as residents and the public, can be improved.

Risk and penal policy in the 1990s

The assessment and management of risk is high on the agenda of the Probation Service in the late 1990s and penal policy generally. In the wake of public anxiety abut the risk of 'dangerous' offenders and the inability of the criminal justice system to deal adequately with those who commit crime, the government has responded through the publication of policy documents including *Crime, Justice and Protecting the Public* (Home Office, 1990) and *Protecting the Public - The Government's Strategy on Crime in England and Wales* (Home Office, 1996), and legislation such as the Criminal Justice Act (1991). *National Standards for the Supervision of Offenders in the Community* (Home Office, 1992; 1995; 2000) has been produced which specifically relates to the work of the Probation Service. The impact of these policies and legislative changes has resulted in greater attention to procedures for identifying and regulating the risk posed by offenders to the public. The concern with the prediction of risk has always been present within the criminal justice system. Indeed, this has formed the basis of parole decision making since its introduction (Maguire, 1992). What has changed is the social, economic and political climate in which the assessment and management of risk takes place.

As other authors have argued, notably Kemshall (1995, 1998), the assessment and management of risk forms one aspect of the 'new penology' (Feeley and Simon, 1992). Feeley and Simon suggest that the new penology is neither about punishing nor rehabilitating individuals. Instead, it is about identifying and managing unruly groups. The major emphasis is on aggregate groups rather then individuals, and on the management of crime opportunities rather than criminals *per se* (Kemshall and Maguire, 2000). Faced with the difficulty of scarce resources, the response has been to target these increasingly limited resources on those considered the most risky to public safety. For those deemed to be less risky, community penalties should be utilised in order to diminish prison overcrowding and to reduce prison costs. The new managerial discourse thus comprises actuarial language of probabilistic calculations and statistical distribution applied to populations. Within the context of England and Wales, this new penology has co-existed alongside a political desire to be 'tough' on offenders and a belief that 'prison works'. The 1991 Criminal Justice Act incorporated the bifurcatory policy which Feeley and Simon discuss, widening the range of community penalties available to sentencers; yet it gave these new penalties a punitive dimension (Cavadino and Dignan, 1997). The consequence of the above was to give the Probation Service a greater role than ever before in terms of responsibility for identifying and managing risk posed by offenders at particular points in their interaction with the criminal justice system. These included the sentencing stage, during supervision in the community and when releasing offenders from prison. Indeed Kemshall (1998) describes risk as the core business of the Probation Service: a central focus of practitioner activity and a key area of scrutiny and accountability for managers.

Risk and approved bail and probation hostels

The role of bail and probation hostels has changed somewhat over the past twenty years (see chapter two). The decline of the rehabilitative ideal (Cavadino and Dignan, 1997), problems of under-occupancy within hostels, high levels of unemployment amongst hostel residents and a growing remand population in the 1980s and 1990s have resulted in a change of direction for approved hostels. Approved hostels now tend to be used more for those on bail, with bailees making up on average 62 percent of hostel residents in 1997/8 (HM Inspectorate of Probation, 1998). Similarly, the four hostels included in this study were all bail and probation hostels but on average at least two-thirds of the residents were waiting for trial. Whilst approved hostels are still used for those on probation, they can only accommodate those charged with offences deemed serious enough under the terms of the 1991 Criminal Justice Act (Osler, 1995). In this respect, the assessment and management of risk assumes a greater role than ever before.

The current edition of *National Standards* states that the purpose of approved hostels is to provide 'an enhanced level of residential supervision with the aim of protecting the public by reducing the likelihood of offending' (Home Office, 2000; Section E.1; see Appendix B). It makes it clear that approved hostels should not simply be used as an accommodation resource, rather to provide a supportive and structured environment. Outlined in *National Standards* (Home Office, 2000) is an admission policy. Each hostel is expected to develop their own policy although ultimate decisions about who should reside in approved hostels as a condition of a bail or probation order are the responsibility of the criminal courts. *National Standards* states that hostel admissions should be based on risk assessment procedures and emphasises that no category of offence is automatically excluded. The risk assessment procedure should identify risk of serious harm to the public, hostel staff, the individual or other hostel residents; and reflect the ability of the hostel to manage and reduce risk identified in accordance with local public protection policies and practices and to reduce the likelihood of offending. Within *National Standards*, what constitutes 'risk' is not explicitly specified even though the assessment of risk is seen as a vital part of the decision-making process

74

in relation to prospective residents. The complex character of risk makes it difficult to define and predict. However, as other have noted (Kemshall, 1995), within Probation Service documentation, risk is often seen as synonymous with dangerousness and referred to almost exclusively as acts of potential physical or sexual violence. Within hostel settings, the assessment of risk may be concerned with risk in terms of property crime, bullying, spread of disease, arson, suicide and self-harm and substance use, although the focus of this chapter is on risk in relation to violence, broadly defined. The discussion which follows explores the difficulties of assessing risk in relation to prospective residents.

The referral process

Referrals to approved hostels are usually made by probation officers or bail information staff, sometimes working in prisons, although at Victoria House a member of staff visited a women's prison on a weekly basis to allow women prisoners the opportunity to self-refer. Normally referrals are taken over the telephone and decisions are made collectively between assistant managers, seeking the advice of the manger or deputy manager if available. The difficulty hostel staff faced was attempting to make an assessment about risk based on as much information as possible within a short space of time.

> There is a lot to think about and yes you feel you are making those decisions very quickly. The pressure from the court duty officer is that they want a decision. The pressure from us is that we want the full information to be able to make that decision.
>
> (Deputy manager, Victoria House)

> I think that [the local] probation service have asked the hostels department to have a fifteen minute turnaround. We could do that for standard, straightforward referrals but where there are mental health issues or where there are incidents of violence on record or drug use, that's a bit more complicated to give an answer so quickly.
>
> (Manager, Victoria House)

The manager of Victoria House, quoted above, suggests some of the issues which need to be considered when a referral is taken which forms the basis of a risk assessment. Each hostel has a referral form and a standard list of questions is asked about every potential resident. The main issues include offence charged with or convicted of, previous convictions, drug and alcohol problems, mental health problems, any history of violence and so forth. Often this information was not readily available. One of the main difficulties was obtaining sufficient knowledge on which to make a 'good enough decision' (Tallant and Strachan, 1995, p.203). Some hostel workers felt that in a small number of cases, field probation officers were unwilling to consider the risks posed by their clients when placed in a residential setting. For instance,

> Some referrals we get . . . referring agents, usually probation officers, might not have thought them through or interviewed them properly. They refer them here because they are desperate for a place for the woman. It hasn't really been looked into well enough and it's a totally different set of issues to what we've first been told.
>
> (Assistant manager, Victoria House)

The comment above alludes to a number of difficulties faced by hostel workers. Field probation officers and hostel workers may vary in their views about what constitutes risk. Probation officers need to appreciate the risk presented by those they refer in the context of a residential rather than a field setting. This is difficult because probation officers in the field may spend little time with their clients and may feel safe because they have meet them in a probation office with people around and good levels of security. A more cynical view was expressed by a small number of hostel workers that in a small number of instances, information available is not passed on to enable a hostel place to be secured. This then puts them as members of staff at risk, as well as other residents and the public, and reinforces the view that hostel work is seen as low status and thus forms an adjunct to mainstream probation practice. Ideally, hostel workers would prefer to verify information received. Faced with the reality of the practical constraints of imperfect knowledge and lack of time, hostel staff have to make 'good enough' decisions rather than 'perfect' decisions (Tallant and Strachan, 1995, p.202-203).

Each hostel had a small number of categories of residents they were unwilling to accept. For instance, Harding House was unwilling to accept sex offenders in order to prevent bullying within the hostel and to protect the local community. Carlton House would not take those charged with, or convicted of, offences which were against children. Other categories of clients such as drug users were not excluded but managers emphasised the need to consider the mix of people in the hostel at any one time.

> If we've got - we don't put numbers on drug users and say we've got four drug users so we aren't going to accept any more. But we look at the chaos of the house, four of five drug users who are more or less stable but two who are really quite chaotic, then to bring another drug user in at that time is probably not going to be helpful to any of those we've currently got here or to that person. So we say no at the moment due to hostel mix, but perhaps in a months time.
>
> (Deputy manager, Victoria House)

The 1998 inspection also found that some hostels were placing a ceiling on the number of drug misusers who could be resident in a hostel at any one time, sometimes set by the hostel's GP (HM Inspectorate of Probation, 1998). Staff at Carlton House and North Street Hostel commented on the need to consider the resident mix too, but also emphasised the flexibility which characterised the decision-making process. For example, given a concentration of drug users in the hostel, they would consider another if they were committed to giving up and could be linked in with a community-based treatment programme. The difficulty here is that prospective residents sometimes agreed to this course of action in order to avoid a custodial remand or sentence but continued with their substance use upon arrival at the hostel. Such residents cannot be compelled to attend such programmes and in any case, community-based treatment programmes have traditionally been unwilling to work with those who lacked a commitment to at least harm reduction. The introduction of the Drug Treatment and Testing Order may enforce a rethinking of this attitude. They could only be breached if in default of hostel rules, for instance by bringing illegal drugs on to the hostel premises.

Despite taking a wide range of factors into account, the four hostels studied appeared to be willing, where possible, to accept those referred and only in exceptional circumstances would an individual be refused. To illustrate,

> You work from a position of saying yes.
>
> (Deputy manager, North Street Hostel)

Well for one thing the rule is you don't ever say no without consulting somebody else. In the last month we've refused one in July and we refused one in June. That's the level we are working at.

(Manager, Carlton House)

At Carlton House, as at other hostels (see HM Inspectorate of Probation, 1998), assistant managers were empowered to accept referrals but not to refuse them without seeking advice from a senior colleague. Hence, as far as possible, hostels tried to accept those at risk of custody provided that the safety of other residents, staff and the public was not placed in jeopardy. They were willing to take those charged with, or convicted of, serious offences with multiple and complex problems. Inevitable, such residents pose a certain level of risk although one which hostel staff felt could be managed. Care was taken to prevent the use of hostel accommodation for low risk individuals who could be dealt with by other means, thus avoiding a process of net-widening which some researchers have suggested has occurred; in other words, hostels accommodating those who would have previously got bail without a condition of residence rather than those at risk of being remanded into custody (see chapter one).

Such decisions are made in a difficult context. An important pressure acting upon hostel staff, particularly managers and deputy managers, is the pressure to maintain the Home Office occupancy targets. The women-only hostels struggled to maintain high levels of occupancy which is surprising given the lack of hostel accommodation for women. This situation, as the above comments from the manager at Carlton House illustrate, was not the consequence of applying strict eligibility criteria or a lack of referrals rather an unwillingness on behalf of the courts to use hostel accommodation for women. In addition, it was difficult for staff at North Street Hostel to fill beds for women. At this hostel, under-occupancy was attributed to a lack of referrals, mainly caused by the unwillingness of some referrers to place women in mixed-hostels. In contrast, the beds for men at North Street Hostel and Harding House could be filled with relative ease. The pressure to maintain occupancy creates was illustrated vividly by the manager at Carlton House:

You walk in in the morning and look at the board, go straight up there and ask how many have we got in. That is the pressure because you know that everybody, every single body you have in, brings in income.

78

This is the context in which risk assessment in relation to potential residents takes place. The need to maintain high occupancy rates does not sit easily with other concerns of hostel managers and other staff. The need to balance competing demands was evident in the accounts of hostel managers and deputy managers.

> I'm always aware of the need to keep a balance in the hostel of women with severe addiction problems and those without. That can be problematic and of course we are always battling for occupancy and that doesn't fit neatly with full occupancy.
>
> (Manager, Victoria House)

> There is a pressure to keep occupancy rates up. That's a pressure which hostel managers carry and staff see if from the other side: 'We have to sleep here. We have to deal with the problems'. So it creates pressure within the hostel too.
>
> (Deputy manager, Victoria House)

What has been illustrated is the difficulties of maintaining full occupancy at the same time as showing concern for potential and actual residents, members of staff, the public and the smooth running of the hostel. The pressure to maintain occupancy is immense particularly as failure to meet occupancy target may result in less funding in the short-term and closure in the long-term. Risk assessments take place in the context of conflicting pressures and staff are left with uneasy decisions to make. The consequences of inadequate risk assessment at this early stage can be extreme. If nothing else, it leads to greater difficulties in managing tension and conflict within the hostel.

Managing 'trouble'

> Hostels assembled anxious, disorganised, bored and despondent individuals . . . There was much potential violence . . . The volatility of individuals who were living by order of the court with strangers under similar constraints, was not necessarily predictable from the pattern and nature of previous convictions. Inflammatory incidents suddenly exploded, apparently with warning, often in response to a seemingly minor irritation . . . Staff had to be constantly vigilant,

alert to mood and atmosphere and willing to intervene to defuse confrontations between residents.

(HM Inspectorate of Probation, 1993, p.25)

There are placid bits, explosive bits and riotous bits. It's very organic.

(Assistant manager, Harding House)

Bail and probation hostels offer accommodation to a wide variety of people of different ages, ethnicities, nationalities, social classes and sexualities. Whilst some residents may be accustomed to institutions such as hostels, other residents may never have been in contact with the criminal justice system before. Added to the pressures generated from sharing relatively cramped living conditions and the anxieties amongst bailees - the majority of residents - which flow from waiting for trial, living in a hostel is not easy. Violence did not appear to be a common occurrence, but there were many other examples of tension and conflict. During the fieldwork, a number of examples of tension and conflict were witnessed. These ranged from the seemingly trivial (although important to the individuals at the time) including arguments over the television, noise and taking clothes out of the washing machine through to problems relating to residents being breached, the discovery that one resident was charged with offences against children, needles being left around in the hostel and bullying.

Inevitably within hostels, staff were not always aware of the potential for trouble. Given the unpredictability of individuals in the resident group, a volatile situation could arise at any moment without warning, posing a risk to the safety of residents and staff. In addition, the design of the hostels made it difficult to be aware of everything that was going on. The four hostels in which this research took place, like many hostels, were not purpose built. They were converted houses or commercial buildings. Three of the four hostels had been created out of what was originally more than one building. Consequently, incidents might be taking place in part of the hostel, unbeknown to staff. However, the solution to this was not to increase surveillance through 'policing' the hostel or through technological means. Staff were conscious of the need to balance security measures with a concern for the privacy of hostel residents (see Wincup, 2001a). Sometimes, the need to manage risk has to be prioritised. For example, at Carlton House, staff became aware that men were entering the hostel in the middle of the night. The 'code' amongst residents prevented what they termed 'grassing'. Thus, staff as a last resort sometimes conducted room checks during the night. This was felt necessary to protect other residents and their children. The consequences of this was great animosity between staff and residents, as well as amongst the resident group who felt that their privacy had been infringed as a result of the acts of others which put them at risk. The management of risk takes places in a setting where the need to maintain constructive relationships and provide a temporary 'home' as far as possible is paramount.

The next section draws heavily on the accounts of hostel workers and explores their feelings of safety and vulnerability.

Vulnerable workers?

In recent years, it has been recognised that bail and probation hostels are risky places to live and work. The introduction of double cover in 1992 has avoided the situation where one member of staff was left alone to manage the hostel, usually at times when incidents of violence were most likely to occur, for example, at night time. Having at least two members of staff available at all times allows incidents to be more satisfactorily contained and reduces feeling of vulnerability amongst individual workers. This view was shared by two members of staff interviewed at Harding House who had experiences of working in bail and probation hostels work prior to the introduction of double.

> Now with double manning life is so much easier. You don't have to keep constantly looking over your shoulder to see if someone else is there. I think it is quite essential in this environment because there is the potential for violence.
>
> (Assistant manager, Harding House)

> It was quite scary to be honest. The sleeping room at that time was upstairs and every bump and bang you heard, you would think what's that?
>
> (Assistant manager, Harding House)

However, as other practitioners have noted (Anon, 1993), the presence of Another person on site does not go the full distance towards taking account and care of the health, safety and well-being of staff. More needs to be done and suggestions for change are explored later in this chapter. At the very least there is a need to ensure that double cover is provided at all times. One member of staff interviewed in 1995, three years after the introduction of double cover, suggested that this was not the case.

> There is not double cover all the time, early morning for example. There are gaps in the rota. Today there was a half hour gap before the evening worker came in, so if she had been stuck in traffic I'm sat here on my own with a hostel full of women and anything could happen. I'm very aware of that. You are so vulnerable.
>
> (Assistant manager, Victoria House)

The introduction of double cover resulted in the need for extra resources for staff to be allocated to hostels. As the manager at Carlton House explained, these resources had not been provided and thus the effectiveness of double cover was substantially reduced.

> What we did then [prior to 1992] was to have four assistant managers who covered the hostel on single cover every day, permanent members of staff, fully trained and familiar with the routines. Then we went to double cover and what we were doing then was having an extra person on duty who was a relief member of staff, who would come and go and who didn't have training . . . It was an emergency measure to cover the double cover which came in overnight . . . four years later that emergency provision still exists . . . If you've got a permanent member of staff ill or on holiday, you've got two reliefs on . . . It's totally unacceptable.
>
> (Manager, Carlton House)

Despite the introduction of double cover, the majority of staff still reported feeling vulnerable, at least at particular times at work. Whilst staff were aware than violent incidents were rare, all were attuned to their vulnerability. Typical comments included: 'you're so vulnerable' (Assistant manager, North Street Hostel) and 'it's a very risky job' (Assistant manger, North Street House). However, it was also noted that it was perhaps even riskier for those who live in hostels. These views are based on their feeling that the potential for violence is always there.

> It's a bit disconcerting sometimes. There is always the fear of something happening . . . I suppose at the back of your mind it is

there but I don't think I am ever consciously scared or whatever. You just hope that nothing will happen but the potential is always there. You have to be mindful of that.

(Assistant manager, Harding House)

I might get stabbed tomorrow or bashed on the head, hopefully not. The potential for that exists. It's there but not that real, You can't let it go. You are constantly aware of the potential there but being aware reduces the risk.

(Assistant manager, Harding House)

Coping with feelings of vulnerability can be a difficult task for staff new to residential work with offenders. This is illustrated vividly by the comment below from a young woman, relatively new to hostel work, with little experience of working with offenders.

If I started thinking I was unsafe it would drive me mad so I just sort of pretend that it's all safe. I'm sure that it isn't but I don't dwell on that too much. I'd rather go along in my own magical world thinking that I'm going to be OK . . . Most of the time it's alright and I think no-one is going to break my door down and come in in the middle of the night. Well they might do but you try and convince yourself otherwise.

(Assistant manager, North Street Hostel)

Coping was also difficult for those who had previously worked with offenders. For example, the two ex-police officers employed at Harding House noted that they were used to dealing with confrontation. However, one of these still felt vulnerable when faced with situations peculiar to residential work, for example, sleeping-in. Additionally, the manager at Victoria House, an experienced senior probation officer, emphasised the additional vulnerability encountered by hostel staff. In contrast to probation offices, hostels do not have alarm systems and other security measures, and sometimes few people are around. This has consequent implications for safety and feelings of security. Those interviewed suggested that as time progressed and they built up practice experience, they felt more able to cope with feelings of vulnerability.

You become more comfortable with handling problems, violence whatever, as time goes on even though there is throughput and the hostel is constantly changing . . . It bothered me a lot at first. I kept

looking over my shoulder but you become more comfortable with it.
You learn to read situations I suppose.

(Assistant manager, Harding House)

Not only were staff aware of the potential for violence, but they were aware of the particular situations which could lead to violence and, in the words of the assistant manager just quoted were able to read these situations. As noted above, this is a skill which has to be acquired by those new to hostel work. This involved knowledge of times of the day when violence could occur, usually at curfew time (11pm) which coincides with closing time from public houses. Staff also emphasised in their accounts the importance of alcohol and drug use in generating behaviour which could lead to violence.

> We have an 11 o'clock curfew. In they come, 2 or 3 of them tanked up and they just want to be the boys as it were and that's when it becomes explosive.
>
> (Assistant manager, Harding House)

> It's especially if someone comes back drunk. You can get a great guy and drink changes him just like that. They become very argumentative.
>
> (Assistant manager, Harding House)

> Particularly with drink, people's behaviour changes: they become aggressive and that can have an impact on the whole house. I've been here just over a year and I can tell if there is going to be trouble by how it feels. You come in and you can feel the tension if there are a lot of drinkers or drug users in the house. So a couple of weeks ago, I could feel that building up and somebody was breached at the weekend and that was drug-related.
>
> (Assistant manager, Victoria House)

The final comment from the assistant manager at Victoria House raises an issue emphasised by other workers. They were aware of the potential for trouble but could not always articulate the causes of it, or know exactly when the problems will arise. However, by being 'alert to mood' (HM Inspectorate of Probation, 1993, p.25) they could intervene when necessary to stop the severity of the incident escalating and pass on this information to staff coming on for the next shift. The latest thematic inspection of hostels (HM Inspectorate of Probation, 1998) praised this aspect of hostel work.

> Inspectors were impressed by the way in which most staff were able to demonstrate their alertness in identifying potential triggers and danger signs, often expressed in changes in mood or attitude as well as the behaviour of residents.
>
> (HM Inspectorate of Probation, 1998, p.86)

Hostel staff talked about this awareness in terms of a 'gut reaction' or 'sixth sense'. Drawing upon the work of Schon (1983), this can be described sociologically as 'tacit knowledge-in-action'. Professionals in their everyday work display skills for which they cannot state the rules or procedures. They are known but cannot be articulated. This knowledge base derives mainly from previous personal and professional experiences. Also part of this tacit knowledge is an awareness that some extreme situations could not be handled by hostel workers, for example, uncontrollable anger, and in those situations staff would try to avoid confrontation and protect themselves by locking themselves in a room and calling the police.

> Sometimes you can't handle it and you have to call the police to take that person away. That's always a bit of a failure. You feel like you've lost that one.
>
> (Night support worker, Harding House)

> Last night when I was dealing with a young woman who we don't know but she's exhibiting bizarre behaviour and there may be a mental health issue there, but there might not; it could be play acting. In situations like that if I feel I'm at risk at all I'm not taking any chances. When I went through a whole system of negotiation and trying to find out what was the matter and it wasn't working and I still felt uneasy about it, I came into the office and locked the door. I've got no compunction about doing that but its not nice.
>
> (Night support worker, Victoria House)

Only one of the twenty members of staff interviewed reporting experiencing serious violence. Part of her detailed account is reproduced below.

85

We took one woman when I'd just started, maybe three months in, and she'd only been here for a few nights and one night she went mad. She jumped out of the back window, trying to kick the door down, running around, smashing things. I was locked in the office. She had a knife and was threatening to kill us all. She got into the garden, jumped the fence, kicking the door and all this because she had taken crack.

(Assistant manager, Victoria House)

This is an extreme example but one which illustrates the potential for violence within hostels and the potential for such situations to increase as hostel accommodate a growing number of 'risky' people such as those who are problem drug users or drinkers.

What became clear from the hostel workers' accounts was that individual workers differed in their feelings of vulnerability, reflected in the ways in which they handled situations and followed safety procedures such as carrying alarms (surprisingly, many did not carry alarms with them on a routine basis; only when they felt particularly vulnerable). There appeared to be no apparent differences in the accounts of the female and male staff interviewed (although generalising from such small numbers is difficult). Residential workers, both female and male, provided honest reflections on their feelings of vulnerability. Those who showed greatest concerns about safety appeared to be those who had experienced violent or threatening incidents. For such workers, concerns about safety could be a source of stress and anxiety.

Developing safer hostels to live and work in

Interviews with hostel workers demonstrated not only aspects of good practice in assessing and managing risk, but also insight into how such practices might be developed. The two thematic inspections of approved bail and probation hostels (HM Inspectorate of Probation, 1993 and 1998), particularly the latter, produced recommendations for practice development. In addition, ways of developing safer working practices has been an important theme in the literature on violence in the workplace. The following section draws on these resources and suggests ways to develop safer hostels to live and work in.

86

Within hostels, the need to assess risk begins at the referral stage. The HM Inspectorate of Probation (1998) report provides examples of good practice in individual probation areas which could usefully be extended to all hostels in England and Wales. Firstly, some services had introduced checklists especially for use by referring officers to assist in achieving consistent pre-admission risk assessments. Their aim is to identify the factors which need to be considered in order to determine the level and nature of any risk posed. Applying this scheme in all probation areas would help to overcome some of the difficulties noted in this chapter, particularly differing conceptions of risk held by residential and field workers and insufficient information to inform the assessment process. Secondly, in a number of hostels, it was standard practice for the deputy manager (usually a trained probation officer) to conduct a risk assessment as part of the induction process. This has the advantage of allowing a more considered assessment of risk but also allowing the assessment of risk to be the first stage in an ongoing risk management process, separate from the decision of suitability for a hostel place. The latest version of *National Standards* states that a written risk assessment is required and advocates the use of structured assessment tools (Home Office, 2000). These tools have a number of advantages including a consistent assessment of offending needs (see Chapman and Hough, 1998, p.24 for further discussion of this issue). However, one major problem attached to these use of these tools is that they have been developed on the male population and have not been validated for women (Hannah-Moffatt and Shaw, 2000).

The 1998 inspection report argued for the formalisation of procedures already operating in the four hostels studied. It prioritised written risk assessment, action plans, regular reviews and the collation of information about risk. Whilst this may be regarded by some as unnecessary bureaucracy, it serves a key role in the risk assessment and management process by providing evidence of 'defensible decisions' (Kemshall, 1998). In other words, if things goes wrong and hostels are held accountable for their actions, evidence is offered of the steps taken to assess and manage the risk posed by a particular individual. Thus it serves as a helpful management tool. More crucially it acts as a practice tool which encourages quality assurance and thorough risk assessments based on evaluations of all the evidence available.

Given the nature of the client group accommodated in hostels, risk becomes something to be managed on a day-to-day basis. There are solid foundations in relation to this aspect of hostel work on which to develop good practice. Both the 1993 and 1998 inspections praised the role played by hostel workers in minimising the risk posed by residents. However, a more proactive approach could be taken in terms of developing the skills and knowledge of workers in this area through training courses, complemented by staff supervision. Given that risk decisions are rarely made in isolation and the centrality of teamwork (see chapter four) to good risk management, attention should be given in team meetings to review assessments, monitor risk management and evaluate the effectiveness of interventions.

Despite the attention to risk assessment and management, on some occasions hostel workers may still experience violence or threats of violence. There is a need for greater attention to be paid to developing the skills of workers to handle such situations.

> When I was telling you about the woman who went mad, that happened when I was quite new and there was a relief member of staff on waking night who hadn't a clue and neither did I. My response was to lock myself in the office and phone the police . . . The relief worker said let's go and calm her down. It wasn't that kind of anger that you felt confident challenging . . . It was an awful situation made worse by the fact that I was supported by someone who didn't have a clue and would have done all the wrong things. I found out that I did exactly the right thing.
>
> (Assistant manager, Victoria House)

The above comment provides convincing evidence for the development of training programmes for all staff who work in hostels, including relief workers, as soon as they begin work in hostels. However, this has to be backed up by appropriate support if a staff member becomes the victim of violence.

> When it was over and they'd arrested her and taken her away, there was blood and glass everywhere and I cleaned it all up. There was no way I could go back to bed and sleep and by the time people came in, it was like I'd held myself together for so long and I was like yes it was bad, no I don't want counselling and let's keep going. When I went home I did actually got to bed but I kept waking up, convinced that someone was trying to get into my bedroom window. I came back to work but the access to counselling wasn't there.

Her recommendation was that the Probation Service should provide access to counsellors for staff, who they could drop in to see or telephone to make an appointment. Other practitioners have offered alternative suggestions. Anon (1993), reflecting on her own experiences of being attacked in a hostel and the lack of support following the attack, suggested the following: providing space to explore the emotional consequences of victimisation and practical offers of support, for example by swapping shifts to allow distance following an attack. Attention to these issues at hostel, local probation area and Home Office level is urgently needed.

Concluding comments

This chapter has explored the process of assessing and managing risk in bail and probation hostels. Through focusing on two aspects of hostel work: the referral process and the management of trouble, some of the dilemmas relating to the assessment of management of risk have been highlighted. The particular social, economic and political climate in which hostel staff now work and the unique characteristics of residential work with offenders which give risk assessment and management a particular accent have been outlined. The assessment and management of risk permeates every aspect of work with offenders in residential setting such as bail and probation hostels. There is a need for both proactive action to be taken to reduce the likelihood of violence complemented by policies which outline procedures, including the provision of support for staff if violence should occur.

The need to develop better systems to assess and manage risk is likely to continue as a priority for hostels. Risk management is now perceived as a necessary precondition of effective practice. As scarce resources under the 'new penology' become targeted at the most risky groups, the future for hostels may lie in working with high risk offenders. Hostels have already begun to diversify for example taking prisoners on home leave who are viewed as 'too risky' to be unsupervised; for example, sex offenders. Alternatives measures may be used for some of the client group traditionally accommodated in hostels, for example, electronic monitoring. Whilst current practice and procedures appear generally to work, developing procedures for assessing and managing risk appears crucial. As Kemshall (1996) notes, a way forward is to increase the knowledge base of hostel workers about risk and ground that knowledge in practice experience and practice wisdom. This involves encouraging hostel staff to evaluate in practice (Shaw, 1996), to do explicitly what is already done implicitly and reflect individually and as a team on the process of risk assessment and management in order to encourage best practice.

6 Unrelenting Stress? Surviving Residential Work

Exposure to stress at work is gradually becoming recognised as a potentially damaging human condition since prolonged or intense stress[1] can lead to mental and physical ill health. The Health and Safety Executive (2001) argues that stress-related illnesses are responsible for the loss of 6.5 million working days each year, costing employers around £370 million and society as a whole as much as £3.75 billion. An estimated half a million people in Britain are thought to be suffering from work-related stress, anxiety or depression at levels them make them ill. In Britain today work-related stress is the second most common type of ill health. One in five people report their work as 'very' or 'extremely' successful. The causes of stress are very varied but in popular discourse stress at work has been linked to major changes in the workplace and the perceived deterioration in home and working lives (Balloch et al, 1998). Long hours, increasing workloads and job insecurity have all been cited as factors producing what is variously known as workplace, occupational or job stress.

Over the past two decades stress has become the focus of many academic studies covering occupations as diverse as policing (Brown and Campbell, 1994), teaching (Ostell and Oakland, 1995) and caring for individuals with HIV/AIDS (Miller, 200), an academic journal entitled *Work and Stress* has been established, and a plethora of self-help books have been published. A growing number of research studies have focused on the workplace experiences of employees in the social services, particularly social workers (see for example Balloch et al, 1998; Bennett et al, 1993).

Defining stress

At its simplest, stress can be defined as a symptom of some sort of pressure. The Health and Safety Executive (HSE) define work-related stress as the adverse reaction people have to excessive pressure or other types of demands placed upon them. This definition differentiates between the beneficial effects of stretching and challenging work which can provide a 'buzz' leading to stimulation, heightened curiosity and an energetic approach to work, and work-related stress which can ultimately lead to breakdown. This is often referred to in social work discourse as 'burnout' (Cherniss, 1980; Maslach, 1980; Pines et al, 1981). However, the HSE definition treats stress at work as a problem which can be tackled in isolation, and implies that the public sphere of work can be separated from the private sphere of home. It does not explicitly recognise that stress can stem from a number of sources.

Brown and Bourne (1996) identify four primary systems relevant to social workers, and suggest that stress can stem from these different sources. Firstly, stress many originate from the personal life of a worker and include problems such as relationship difficulties, financial problems or a bereavement. Secondly, stress may emanate from practice in two main ways. It may be a consequence of victimisation in the form of physical assault, oppressive verbal abuse of threats of violence. Stress may also result from the experiences of others which stir up strong feelings for the workers including disclosure of abuse and residents with multiple and complex problems, particularly if they relate to difficulties which have also been experienced by the worker. Thirdly, stress may also emanate from membership of a team in a number of ways. This might include personal conflicts with other team members, feelings of isolation within the team and involvement with other colleagues' work stress. Finally, stress may derive from membership of an agency, in this case the Probation Service, and can relate to reorganisation, threats of closure and redundancies and difficulties of achieving promotion. The following discussion of the hostel workers accounts demonstrates that stress experienced by residential workers stemmed from different sources and there are may parallels with the typology offered by Brown and Bourne (1996).

A useful working definition of stress is offered by Lazarus and Folkman (1984). They argue that stress is a result of interactions between environmental demands, perceptions of those demands, the coping resources available to the individual and the emotional outcome of those demands. The strength of this definition is that it allows consideration of both social factors and individual differences. Workers experience stress when there is a disparity between the perceived demands made on the individual and their perceived ability to cope with those demands.

Stress and residential workers

Many studies of stress within social service departments have concentrated on the experiences of social workers but there are some exceptions. A recent study by the National Institute for Social Work research unit (Balloch et al, 1998) surveyed four groups of staff, including residential workers, in five local authorities in England. Residential workers, especially those with management responsibilities, were most at risk of stress. For these workers coping with service users' pain and distress was cited as the most stressful aspects of the job. The Inspection of Approved Probation and Bail Hostels which took place in 1993 recognised this fact but noted that it was not always appreciated in the Probation Service.

> Twenty-four hour care, seven days a week of individuals who have not chosen to live together is a complex and demanding task. Recognition of this is long overdue.
>
> (HM Inspectorate of Probation, 1993, p.10)

There was great consensus in the accounts of the hostel workers that working in a hostel was a difficult and demanding job. Many of the hostel workers interviewed talked at length about the stressful nature of their work. However, there were some dissenting voices.

> I don't find it stressful here; not compared to what I am used to [being a police officer]. That may be down to my personality.
>
> (Night support worker, Harding House)

> Because I've done that [worked as a police officer] maybe I can handle the job more easily because it seems less stressful.
>
> (Assistant manager, Harding House)

The hostel workers interviewed varied in the views on how stressful residential work with offenders was. Within this small sample, those who found it the most stressful tended to be young women who worked as assistant managers, particularly in women-only hostels. Those who reported finding it the least stressful were the two men working at Harding House who had previously worked as police officers which they perceived to be a more stressful job.

There was some disagreement amongst staff who found the work stressful concerning whether the stress was relentless. The two comments below illustrate this divide well.

> The other parts outweigh the stress. Stress is not relentless and you are not ground down by it.
>
> (Assistant manager, Harding House)

> It's the unrelenting stress. It's stressful all the time. It's important to remember that our staff work long unsociable hours.
>
> (Deputy manager, Carlton House)

The latter view gives cause for concern since prolonged stress has the most damaging effects on physical and mental health.

One of the greatest sources of stress was the conflicting demands on their time and therefore even though workers tried to plan their shift often the best laid plans had to be rethought. Typical comments by hostel workers included:

> I find it a bit of a strain sometimes if there are lots of things happening and you haven't got time to do the things that you were planning to do.
>
> (Assistant manager, North Street Hostel)

> It's pretty dynamic here. You end up doing a lot of crisis work with people on bail as well as the intensive supervision of people on your caseload.
>
> (Deputy manager, Harding House)

Stevenson and Parsloe's (1978) study of social service teams also found that the lack of predictability was a source of stress and anxiety. This unpredictability makes residential work distinct from many other occupations. The account below recounts a conversation between a hostel worker and his wife who works in a bank which supports this view.

> I said to her [wife] its OK for you. When you've got a problem, you know its going to be the same when you get back. If I've got a problem, I can come back and think it through in the night and I can be back in the next day and it has all disappeared anyway. Either that or you can come away thinking I've done a great days work.

94

Everything is fine in the hostel. Everyone in the hostel loves one another. Everything in the garden is rosy and you can get in at 9 o'clock in the morning and all hell has broken loose in the night. There is that uncertainty about it all. We are dealing with some pretty volatile people. The chances are that all hell will break loose at some point.

(Deputy manager, Harding House)

Adding to the unpredictability of residential work is the sheer diversity of work to be undertaken.

You get everything from people arguing over who has got the most potatoes to someone coming in to the office saying I've cut my wrist. You get everything to deal with.

(Assistant manager, Harding House)

An important argument advanced by hostel workers was that the lack of routine and the diversity of work paradoxically contributed to make hostel work interesting as well as stressful. A common theme was that even if hostel work was perceived as stressful, job satisfaction was still derived, often sometimes from the very sources which led to the stress.

Something that I hate about it but I also really like about is that you are doing something different every day . . . We don't have our own quiet space to get on with work. You are constantly being disturbed every five minutes. Everything is disturbed, even the handover because somebody will ring up with a referral and you have got to drop everything and get on with that. I find it hard when I'm tired, when I've done sleep ins, to cope with everything changing. It is exhausting and can be frustrating but it is sometimes really interesting.

(Assistant manager, North Street Hostel)

The account above refers to the fact that residential workers often work long hours. This was commented on by some members of staff, for example:

Tonight I'm staying here . . . You don't get to bed until 1 or 2 am and you are up at 8am. I've been here since 9.30 am and I'm knackered already and its not even 10pm.

(Assistant manager, Victoria House)

95

Often the physical conditions did not accord them much privacy or comfort when they took their breaks or were doing sleep ins.

> The staff room, the sleeping room - I don't think it's as comfortable as it could be. You make do a lot. It's a really hard job to do and if you're doing a whole weekend. It would be nice to have a little more comfort than we actually have got. Our staff bedroom doubles up as an interview room, a keyworking room, a meeting room.
>
> (Assistant manager, Victoria House)

In the context of hostels for offenders, it was often difficult to take a break. The requirement to provide double cover at all times meant at weekends and evening when only two staff were in the hostel, it was impossible for a member of staff to go out even for a few minutes. In all four hostels, there was a lack of space and few staff only areas. Consequently, they tended to remain in the office or a communal area and therefore were constantly disturbed as an assistant manager at Victoria House described.

> When you are here you don't get time for a proper break really. I could be eating my dinner and people will come up to me and say I want this, or the phone rings and you've got to go and answer it.

Perhaps most importantly, stress stems from their involvement in resident's problems.

> Throughout the time I've worked here we've had quite a number of women return from buying drugs, or just living in dangerous situations, who've been seriously assaulted. That's the sort of things people bring back. It's very traumatic for staff.
>
> (Deputy manager, Victoria House)

> You are soaking up, taking in, people's emotional problems day after day. There is no respite. The hostel is there all the time.
>
> (Assistant manager, Victoria House).

> The same sort of problems are being presented to us all the time and whilst you work on them at a professional level, there are times when that work is going to affect you. Issues can relate to people's own lives and there are some traumatic things people present to us.
>
> (Deputy manager, Victoria House)

The accounts of hostel workers support Payne and Scott's (1982) conclusion that residential work involves qualitatively different stresses. They argue that residential workers operate within the primary life-space of their clients, and thus workers and their clients may be 'forced' to share their life experiences as they build up close relationships. In contrast to field probation practice, staff may not have huge caseloads but are required to undertake intensive work with residents who are often experiencing periods of crisis in their lives. Consequently, residential work is demanding and workers need to be supported. Intensive group situations lead to individual workers remaining 'vulnerable to the exposure of deep feelings and emotions which are invariably aroused' (p.17). Hostel workers are relating to their clients as professionals, but also as empathetic individuals. Those roles can conflict. For instance,

> I often think for some of the people here - because of the ethos of the hostel and I can see it as good thing protecting the staff and being professional and I wouldn't have it any way. But there are times when you feel like putting your arm around someone if they are in a right old state. They don't have any kind of affection shown to them and it would be completely inappropriate to do that. I find that a bit difficult at times that you can't say to someone 'bloody hell you're in a right old state, what are you going to do about it?' sort of thing. You've got to hold it together from your point of view and I think that means that sometimes we can be a bit stand-offish.
>
> (Assistant manager, North Street Hostel)

Residential workers are thus engaged in emotion work in the sense that they are working with the emotions of the resident group as well as managing their own emotions. Going back to our working definition of stress, in order to manage these environmental demands, coping resources are essential. These are explored in the following section.

Coping strategies

Lazarus and Folkman (1984) identify two broad categories of coping strategies: problem and emotion-focused. The former involves engaging in behaviours likely to manage the problem that is causing the stress. The latter involves a number of strategies which attempt to regulate aversive emotions or distress which may result from the stressor. These may involve distancing and gathering social support. Those working with offenders in residential settings often felt unable to deal with the problems causing the stress which they felt where part and parcel of the work and thus tended to use emotion-focused strategies. One strategy to cope with the emotional demands of the work is to create emotional distance in an attempt to avoid becoming enmeshed in the concerns of residents. As Bennett et al (1993) discovered, this distancing technique is widely used by social workers. Whilst this technique was discussed by the residential workers, the main coping mechanism they discussed were their attempts to 'switch off' at the end of their shift, in other words attempting to maintain a distinction between home (perceived as their 'refuge') and work.

Residential workers talked in their interviews about the need to divide the private world of home and the public world of work. Sometimes they found it difficult to avoid taking their work home with them, not in a literal sense, but in terms of going home 'heavy and weary'.

> You need the super ability to leave your job here and go home. It's very important because then you are able to deal with things better. It can be tiring and wearing and you leave the hostel stressed and angry.
>
> (Assistant manager, Victoria House)

> Its important for any probation work that you don't take it home. This is not my life. This is what I do for a living.
>
> (Deputy manager, Harding House)

> I've always made it a rule, even in my other occupation [previously a police officer] that when I come to work I close the door on the house and come to work and work. When I leave in the morning I close that door and go home. It's finished. You've got to do that or you can't cope . . . You certainly can't carry it home with you or it would just bother you all day and night.
>
> (Night support worker, Harding House)

> The other thing about probation work generally is that you get to see a lot of other people's misery. You need to try and switch off . . . it's difficult . . . you can't get away from it.
>
> (Deputy manager, Harding House)

As the latter two accounts illustrate clearly this attempt to separate emotionally the spheres of work and home are difficult to put into practice.

Sociological research has illustrated the artificiality of the public/private dichotomy (Garmanikow et al, 1983; Morris and Lyon, 1996), particularly for women. For example,

> the substance of women's lives is shaped by two worlds of work: the home and the labour market. Thus to treat such realms as independent or to imagine that the 'public' has no connection to the 'private' is to ultimately evade or distort the relation women have to the social world
>
> (Berk, 1980, pp.25-26).

Much of this research has considered the ways in which women's responsibilities in the private sphere impact upon their experiences of the public sphere, particularly in relation to employment (Brannen and Moss, 1991; Hochshild, 1989). This was an issue for some hostel workers. However, what affected them all was the difficulty of drawing boundaries between 'work time' and 'non-work time'. This was heightened because the nature of their work did not allow them to easily draw boundaries. The shifts worked varied from week to week. At times in the hostel, they were between work and non-work, asleep in the hostel but on call. This is described by an assistant manager at Victoria House below.

> Tonight I'm staying here and its hard to cut off at midnight. You don't get to bed until 1 or 2 am and you don't really sleep . . . It might have been quite a peaceful shift but you are still here all the time . . I think sometimes there isn't recognition of that from the managers because they don't do that part of the job. They say it was quiet. You probably had the TV on. I'll have the TV on but I'm not really watching it because I'm at work and anything could happen.

Managers faced a similar difficulty. Although they usually worked from nine to five on weekdays, in some probation areas, an on-call system operated. Whilst valued as a means of supporting hostel staff, for managers, it impinged upon their 'non-work' time.

> I'm on call this week so after 6 o'clock I'll have the mobile phone with me so all the staff from the three hostels [in the probation area] can call me at any time
>
> (Deputy manager, North Street Hostel)

> I'm on call one week in three. It's not easy to forget the hostel because you may have to come back into the hostel. You can't really go out or do anything.
>
> (Deputy manager, Harding House)

In order to provide further support to colleagues often managers tried to make themselves as accessible as possible outside their working hours, even when they were not on call.

> I try to make myself available although I'm not paid to be on-call so there is a discrepancy there really in terms of I can't be available all the time because I need my time off but ensuring that they know if they want me or the deputy the help is there if they need it.
>
> (Manager, Victoria House).

> I'm not on call all the time. If it's someone on my caseload, I often say to staff phone me if there is a problem . . . You can't get away from it really.
>
> (Deputy manager, Harding House)

Residential work provides a number of challenges emotionally. One way to manage the feelings which arise is through seeking support, either formally through supervision or informally from colleagues. Previous studies have shown that this can have a significant effect in mediating the effects of stress (for example, Bennett et al, 1993).

The formal dimension of support: Staff supervision

The formalised way of offering support to colleagues, as in other caring professions, is through supervision. The term 'supervision' is defined and used in different ways by different people (Brown and Bourne, 1996). Supervision can be defined as 'the process of talking, to someone else involved in the same system, about what one is doing, in order to be able to do it better' (Atherton, 1986, p.3). This is a succinct definition but we should add to this that the supervisee is an active participant in the interactional process (Brown and Bourne, 1996). Supervision is usually provided by those in managerial positions for individual workers. However, as Payne and Scott (1982) suggest offering support is only one of the functions of supervision. It also has roles to play in contributing to staff development through the provision of relevant knowledge and skills and through the evaluation of progress. Supervision, thus has an expressive and an instrumental focus. This view has many parallels to staff accounts of supervision.

> We offer supervision to staff. It's looking at the whole area, the sort of professional development and the skills needed for the job. It's looking at how working here leaves a member of staff feeling.
>
> (Deputy manager, Victoria House)

> We get supervision every two weeks. We have a chance to talk about things. It's like a keywork session for staff really. If the deputy has highlighted areas where we can improve our performance, we will talk about that, and any residents you are having real problems with and any residents that you are assessing . . . You get to talk about everything. I quite often talk about being the only black worker and being the only single parent. I talk about that, what is important to me.
>
> (Assistant manager, North Street Hostel)

The above comments suggest ways in which many workers felt that supervision was valuable. It can contribute to their professional development, help them to improve their work with residents and provide an opportunity to talk about issues relevant to them.

Supervision was offered in all four hostels but at Harding House some staff voiced particular concerns about the adequacy of formal supervision offered. For example, one of the assistant managers commented:

> I have talked to people in other hostels and it's much more together on that front [supervision] in other places. Well it appears to be and we appear not to have it. I think we are slowly getting it together.

In all four hostels, staff highlighted some of the number of difficulties associated with supervision.

On a practical level, despite the value attached to supervision, it is not prioritised in terms of the work of the hostel, or in other social work settings (Ash, 1995). Competing demands on staff resources resulted in supervision sessions being cancelled. Whilst workers understood the reasons for this, they still felt it to be unsatisfactory.

You get individual chats with management but they are cancelled if the hostel is busy and there is no-one to cover the office.

(Assistant manager, Carlton House)

Formal support we get hopefully once a fortnight - a supervision session. But like most things, it doesn't often happen. I can understand why with the person who is supposed to be giving me supervision working extremely hard. If I thought I wasn't getting supervision because person was lazy, I'd be pissed off and I'd be begging for it. If someone is busy then I don't like to be pestering them . . . I just don't like to be pestering them.

(Assistant manager, North Street Hostel)

This staff member above alludes to another difficulty associated with supervision. Whilst staff may feel they need support, it can be difficult to reach out and ask for it. This was highlighted by other workers too.

There's been times, certainly in the early days, when I've been finding my feet and been finding it difficult to cope with situations that I've found it difficult to reach out and ask for help.

(Night support worker, Victoria House)

This could be for a number of reasons. Asking for help and support may lead to feelings of incompetence. As others have noted, individual workers may feel that discussion of personal feelings in supervision may encourage the supervisor to perceive them as unprofessional (Ash, 1995) or unable to cope (Pithouse, 1987; Satyamurti, 1981). This is heightened in a formal situation such as a supervision when the person who provides support is also a superior.

I think the unspoken pressure is that it is a difficult job and do you always want to talk to your manager about how the work is affecting you because it's a dual role. I've got two interests here: the interests of the member of staff and the interests of the hostel and they don't always link in together. I think there is a slight fear for staff that if they are not seen as emotionally strong, they are not able to cope with their job.

(Deputy manager, Victoria House)

102

Additionally, as the supervisee's stress increases, they may become defensive and prickly, and this can make it difficult for them to acknowledge their own needs and seek help (Brown and Bourne, 1996).

Supporting the needs of the worker is done in the context of ensuring the hostel runs smoothly. The encouragement of reflective supervision which allows for the consideration of personal feelings has been prioritised by practitioners as a means to encourage reflective practice (Ash, 1995; Schon, 1991) which benefits both workers and clients. For managers, the balancing of needs of the hostel and the worker takes another form too. Whilst the manager has to ensure that the hostel runs smoothly, this has to be done in a non-directive way to respect professional autonomy. This is valued by hostel staff.

> I think the manager is very good, very supportive. I think she is very supportive in the ways she respects her staff team and she does not manage by looking over your shoulder. She trusts her staff team know how to do their job. At the same time, if you are having difficulties the space is there to discuss it with the staff team or the manager without being made to feel that you are incapable, or it's a problem. There is the room there to build on your skills, to actually make use of your skills and be trusted as a worker, and there is room when you are having problems.
>
> (Night support worker, Victoria House)

The findings explored in this chapter have many parallels with the 1998 inspection of approved hostels (HM Inspectorate of Probation, 1998). The inspection team found that there was considerable variation across hostels in terms of arrangements for staff supervision, and that frequently supervisions were cancelled. They also noted the lack of time and opportunities assistant wardens had for debriefing following difficult incidents with residents.

Given the shortcomings associated with supervision, staff tended to develop alternative ways of coping with the effects of residents off-loading on to them and other sources of stress. However, such strategies can be counter-productive.

> You find that by the time it is your appointment for supervision, you've developed your own kind of defence mechanism which is to block out a lot of things so you can't even speak about it in that

103

space. It's not that you've forgotten about it, it's in the back of your mind.

(Assistant manager, Victoria House)

Other approaches were far more productive. In particular, talking to colleagues informally was regarded as a valuable means of emotional support.

The informal dimension: Mutual support

We help each other. We deal with it night and day so we tend to use each other for support

(Assistant manager, Victoria House)

Yeah we do offer a lot of support to each other which is good. You don't get a lot of support from the Probation Service . . . I think you just need to sit down occasionally and sound off.

(Assistant manager, Harding House)

On a daily basis, colleagues can be used as a form of support. Handovers between shifts, for example, provide an opportunity to pass on information about residents and to make decisions. Staff meetings, too, can provide some support. In terms of support beyond this, hostels varied in terms of what they provided. A number of informal support mechanisms were brought to my attention during the research, and heralded by staff as good practice.

- At Victoria House, meetings solely with assistant managers were timetabled. This provided an opportunity to discuss issues without the presence of those in management positions, and therefore the power relations that characterise supervision. Sometimes these took place outside the hostel in an informal setting such as a cafe.
- Also at Victoria House a black worker group had been established which had links with a black worker group for all probation employees in the local area.
- At North Street Hostel and Harding House, outside office hours staff had access to a hostel manager from the local probation area who could be contacted on a mobile phone.

- At North Street Hostel a further measure was to establish a link with the local drugs agency so that support could be provided in terms of being able to discuss experiences of working with drug users.
- At Carlton House, staff sometimes made use of the counsellors who visited the hostel to work with the women residents.

Concluding comments

In this chapter we have explored the accounts of twenty hostel workers and their views on the stressful nature, or otherwise, of their work. The consensus was that residential work with offenders is a stressful occupation. Stress stems from a wide range of factors including competing demands on staff time; the diversity of work to be undertaken; the lack of routine; long hours without a break; and involvement with the problems experienced by the client group. However none of the staff talked about breakdown, or 'burnout' as it is characteristically known in social work. Indeed many discussed how some of the factors which result in stress such as the lack of routine also contribute to making the work interesting.

Given the nature of residential work with offenders perhaps some degree of stress is inevitable but there are a number of ways in which additional support can be offered to residential workers. For example, training in personal stress management techniques could be offered. In the absence of formal support, hostel staff were fairly resourceful in terms of the ways they sought support. However, as we noted in chapter five one worker at Victoria House felt that sufficient support was not provided, except in response to a traumatic situation, in her case a horrific violent incident. She made a strong case for staff access to counsellors.

> I think there are grounds for having access to on-site counselling for the staff. At any point in the day you could actually go to that person to talk, or have somebody to talk to on the phone and who you could say to 'Can you come in tomorrow? I'd like to talk to you'.

Brown and Bourne (1996: 112) state 'we believe that good supervision addresses work-related stress before it occurs'. Given the nature of residential work with offenders, this seems rather idealistic. However a combination of formal supervision and informal social support can play key roles in mediating the effects of stress. This research study has revealed many examples of good practice in relation to the provision of informal support which could be replicated in other hostel settings. In addition to the formal provision of support of supervision, managers should consider ways in which they can facilitate informal support in their own hostel, and the Probation Service as a whole needs to think about the support it offers to those who occupy managerial positions. Often as one ascends the organisational hierarchy, supervision is less likely to be used as a forum for having support needs met or practice issues addressed (Brown and Bourne, 1996). In recognition of this, peer or group supervision could be adopted.

Note

1.   These forms of stress are also referred to as accumulated and traumatic respectively.

7 Residential Work with Female Offenders

Introduction

In this chapter, we will consider the approach developed by female[1] staff in response to the realities of working with women, and examine the ways in which the approach is translated into practice. First, the central ideal-typical elements of the approach will be described, and then the examples of substance use, managing violent relationships and offending behaviour will be used to illustrate how the approach is applied to actual work with female offenders in residential settings.

This chapter will concentrate on working with women, and draw upon research conducted in three of the four hostels (the two women-only and one mixed hostel). The findings of this small-scale study are limited in their ability to discuss in detail the experiences of working with men, although there is a short discussion of possible differences between working with women and men at the end of the chapter. In recent years there has been a growing interest in masculinities. The work of Messerschmidt (1993) has been particularly influential in arguing that crime is a resource for 'doing gender', in other words gender is made meaningful through criminal behaviour. This has implications for practice and as Newburn and Mair (1996, p.3) argue '... it is at least as important to deal with these offenders as men as it is to deal with these men as offenders'. There is a growing interest in the issue of working with men in the fields of social work and criminal justice with a number of recent publications devoted to this issue including Cavanagh and Cree (1996), Newburn and Mair (1996) and Scourfield (1998). To date, there has been little examination of gender issues in relation to residential work with offenders.

Working with women: Elements of the approach

As we explored in chapter three *National Standards for the Supervision of Offenders in the Community* (Home Office, 1995) suggests areas to be worked upon including offending behaviour, employment and accommodation. In some ways, hostel staff felt this was too directive. A strong argument was made that the priority issues affecting the lives of female residents may not be the same as for their male counterparts, in particular responsibility for child care, and that residents should direct the process of change. We will return to this issue later in the chapter but suffice to say now that in all three hostels a key principle underlying their practice was that support offered should be client-led *in response to women's needs*. This was stressed by the deputy manager at North Street Hostel who argued that a period of residence in a hostel provides:

> the opportunity to address some of the stuff highlighted on their
> assessment, some of the reasons why they came to the hostel in the
> first place if they wish to, and I stress if they wish to.

This emphasis on allowing residents to direct their own programme of change was shared by staff in the other two hostels.

> It's about giving them the support they want rather than telling them
> what they want.
>
> (Assistant manager, Victoria House)

> We go through the keyworking session and find out what their
> interests are and work from that . . . Basically, it has to come from
> them.
>
> (Assistant manager, Carlton House)

> It's about supporting the women and doing what they want to do. It's
> about picking up issues which are important for the woman and
> dealing with those.
>
> (Assistant manager, Victoria House)

However, women seemed to be encouraged by staff, wherever possible, to take up the support on offer. When residents identify themselves as facing a particular difficulty, the response of the hostel staff was *to present choices* and allow women to decide whether to take up the support on offer.

> We advise them on what's there and advise them that we are here to help them, but the decision is theirs ... We try and push them to take it up if possible but if they don't want to, there's nothing we can do.
>
> (Assistant manager, Victoria House)

This approach was perceived to be in the best interests of the resident. For those who choose to take up the support on offer, residents are required to select an appropriate course of action. Referring to the example of seeking support to give up drug use, a hostel worker at North Street Hostel described the options to be presented to a particular resident.

> If they did want to do something then I'd want to discuss with them a plan of action, how they wanted to go about it, if they wanted to use outside agencies, if they wanted to do it themselves and then I'd reassess that every so often.

The provision of support could take a number of forms which could be categorised as *practical and emotional support*. At a practical level, staff helped with tasks such a making benefit claims, dealing on behalf of the resident with outside agencies, and assisting individual women to find move-on accommodation. Whilst they did not provide formalised counselling, support at an emotional level was provided by offering a 'listening ear' (Assistant manager, Victoria House), and through *access to a staff team which was always available and approachable*. As an assistant manager at Carlton House suggested this was a crucial dimension of support for the women.

> I think just being here. They are always asking when are you back on duty . . . I think just knowing that somebody is looking out for you.

Workers in other hostels agreed.

> If your keyworker isn't there, there is always another member of staff you can talk to at that moment. Night workers provide twenty four hours with someone to talk to.
>
> (Assistant manager, Victoria House)

Hostel staff are available twenty four hours a day . . . people just simply knock on the door. There is a night supervisor . . . more of a security person but a lot of them come and chat to the night supervisor so there is always somebody here and regular keywork sessions should be offered.

(Assistant manager, North Street Hostel)

In addition, staff tried to engage with the women, to offer some degree of empathy and understanding. This involved *recognition of their social position as women* which was crucial to developing an understanding of the causes of their present problems, and the barriers to solving them. The research revealed both the diversity of life experiences of the women residents, but also common themes within their accounts. These included being charged with a criminal offence, low self-esteem and difficulties that stemmed from their socio-economic position in a patriarchal society. These multiple and complex problems include poverty, homelessness, unemployment, experiences of abuse (emotional, physical and sexual) and sole responsibility for the care of dependant children or adults. Many used substances including illegal drugs, alcohol, prescribed medication and food as a coping mechanism (Wincup, 1999 and 2000a). Other studies of women who have appeared before the courts have also highlighted the complex social problems experienced by women (see for example, Carlen, 1988; Eaton, 1993; Morris et al, 1995).[2]

Practical and emotional support was dispensed at a formal level through the allocation of a keyworker who could provide individual attention and an opportunity for private space to discuss issues. Informally support was provided through access to members of staff throughout the day and night. The hope lying behind this system was that constantly available, ongoing support would be provided for the women. All three hostels had a general office with residents given almost free access to hostel staff during the day and evening. Hostel staff also respected that some women would prefer to establish some level of rapport with an individual worker before discussing their lives in depth. Given that a positive relationship between an individual woman and members of staff appeared to be vital to the support process, the provision of support at a formal and informal level also gave the women the opportunity to talk to members of staff they felt comfortable talking about very personal issues with. From the women's accounts, it became clear that many women had a particular person they would turn to first for help which was not necessarily their keyworker.

110

Essential to the establishment of a positive relationship between staff and residents was *the treatment of residents with respect.*

> The main thing is around showing people respect . . . giving them a feeling that they are not useless people.
>
> (Deputy manager, Victoria House)

> I don't hope to be everyone's best friend, but as far as possible I hope to be approachable with people. I hope that as we are with them twenty four hours a day that we are decent to them, because a lot of them have been around people who aren't decent to them and it might help restore their faith somewhere along the line.
>
> (Assistant manager, North Street Hostel)

Linked with treating residents with respect is taking responsibility for women in need, rather than 'passing the buck or saying I can't be bothered to deal with that' (Deputy manager, Victoria House). This is demonstrated by a willingness to accept referrals from women charged with very serious offences with multiple problems to 'give them a second chance' (Manager, Carlton House). Moreover, it involves supporting them when they do not succeed at making changes to their lives.

> If a woman fails tomorrow, It's not my job to say you've done this, you're stupid, you've done this you've failed - forget it. It's my job to say to them, another day, another try.
>
> (Deputy manager, Victoria House)

Whilst staff were willing to provide practical and emotional support, at the same time, women were expected to take responsibility for their own lives. The approach therefore involved *working with the women for the women.* Staff made it clear that the women should direct the process of making changes to their lives supported by staff and to move from situations of crisis to situations in which they were able to establish control over their lives.

> Support is OK but you've got to balance it with people taking charge of their own lives. We tend to act as facilitators, to say what the different agencies are but letting people make their own appointments and keeping them.
>
> (Assistant manager, Carlton House)

111

> The women are here on bail and part of the criteria is for them not only to take responsibility for their actions but also responsibility for their own lives.
>
> (Assistant manager, Victoria House)

> We can do so much for them but if we hold their hands too often and they just rely on that but it doesn't work that way . . . To be quite honest, we haven't got the time to keep holding their hands and taking them to X Y Z so we have to say look here is the phone, here is the address, here is the bus number, make your own steps forward, that sort of thing.
>
> (Assistant manager, Carlton House)

Achieving the delicate balance between encouraging responsibility and providing appropriate levels of support is a difficult task, particularly in a climate of scarce resources. As the last staff member quoted above suggests, one way in which it may be achieved by offering advice and information, suggesting a possible direction forward but allowing the resident the choice whether to follow it up and to have the ultimate responsibility for seeking support.

Whilst hostel staff took responsibility for working with women, often with multiple complex problems, it was necessary to utilise external agencies to a great extent. This was not 'passing the buck' but an essential part of the support process. In order to provide appropriate and constructive support, staff were required *to be conscious of the limitations of their expertise and refer women to more specialist resources*. Staff in all three hostels were conscious of their status as generalist workers rather than specialist professionals.

> We're not specialist in anything. We are the first point of contact. We can give advice on where to go but we can't actually do anything ourselves. That's why it is important to have those links.
>
> (Assistant manager, Victoria House)

> We have good links and I think you have to maintain that. You are not the experts, that you can only help so much, but there are professionals out there who can do it.
>
> (Deputy manager, Carlton House)

We are not counsellors and cannot take on in-depth work with them which obviously some people need.

(Assistant manager, North Street Hostel)

In some ways, hostel workers conveyed a sense of powerlessness in that they were only able to react to the needs of women and offer support in a general rather than specific way. External agencies were therefore utilised to provide support appropriate to the needs of individual women. Hostel staff perceived themselves as a first stage in the process of change but ultimately external agencies needed to be used. This allows the women to have community ties when they leave the hostel. It also involved the need for hostel staff to clearly demarcate the boundaries of their role, to make explicit to women what they could and could not do. This professional and ethical responsibility was described by an assistant manager at North Street Hostel.

I think what you shouldn't do, and you shouldn't set yourself up to be, is someone special who if you are someone's keyworker you are going to do fab things with them.

In summary, the ideal-typical elements of the approach described by staff involved staff aiming to:

Figure 7.1 The ideal-typical approach

1	Respond to the needs of the women.
2	Present choices to the women.
3	Provide practical and emotional support.
4	Be accessible and approachable.
5	Recognise their social position as women and how this impacts on their lives.
6	Treat residents with respect.
7	Work *with* the women *for* the women i.e. taking responsibility for women but at the same time expecting women to take responsibility for their own lives.
8	Be conscious of the limitations of their expertise and refer women to specialist resources when appropriate.

The approach in practice

The approach developed by staff has been outlined in its abstract form. Referring to four case studies, we will now explore some of the ways in which the approach is put into practice around three key issues: substance use, violence within relationships and offending behaviour. The case studies reflect some of the sample's diverse experiences. This is not to claim that any of the cases are typical, nor that their accounts cover all the issues that are pertinent to my analysis of the problems experienced by women resident in approved hostels. However, their stories are not isolated or unusual examples.

Judith was in her early twenties and charged with burglary and breach of bail. She has two young children who she cares for alone. Her previous partners, the fathers of her children, had been violent towards her. Her use of drugs and alcohol in the past had often had a number of negative consequences, leading to her involvement in crime and damaging her health through aggravating her asthma and bringing on anxiety attacks. She had managed to give up illegal drugs and alcohol and is committed to staying off them. She also had a history of depression and found it difficult to deal with the stress of waiting for trial. As a result, she sought medical advice and was prescribed anti-depressants.

Ruth was charged with theft and breach of probation. Despite only being in her early twenties, she had already been convicted of a number of property and violent offences in the past. Before coming into the hostel, she had been sleeping on a series of friends' floors and was unemployed. She had been taking drugs since she was thirteen: cannabis, speed, ecstasy and cocaine but feels she cannot give up while she is in the hostel. She also drank heavily and attended AA sessions. During her stay in the hostel she harmed herself to such an extent that she was taken to the accident and emergency department of the nearby hospital. She described herself as 'screwed up' and noted how she is easily influenced by those she terms the 'wrong' people. Despite her future hopes to continue with her education and perhaps set up her own business, she was pessimistic about the likelihood of giving up substance use and offending in the future.

At 52 *Heather* stood out at Victoria House, not only because of her age, and the seriousness of the offence she has been charged with (murder) but also because she has had no prior involvement with the criminal justice system. After getting divorced in her mid 30s, she met Charlie and he moved into her home. After many experiences of violence linked to his heavy drinking, she retaliated through force and was charged with his murder. This appeared at the time to be her only way out because she felt unable to leave, because she was fearful of his reaction and felt unable to talk to anyone about her life. She was immediately remanded in custody and held on the psychiatric wing, but referred to the hostel by the prison bail unit. She had been waiting trial for several months. Her family visited regularly and were supportive. However, she found it hard to open up and talk about her experiences of violence to the staff who she still regards as strangers, or to her children who she wants to present a particular image to, of someone in control of her life, who is strong-willed and able to cope. Despite the extreme violence she suffered, she wrestled with feelings of guilt and shame. She continued to take tranquillisers to cope with her depression and tablets to enable her to sleep at night. The effects of waiting trial were extreme for her: her health deteriorated, she experienced loneliness and isolation, her rented home was on the verge of being lost and her future was still marked with uncertainty, almost a year after the offence.[3]

Siobhan was 25 and charged with handling stolen property. Initially she was given bail but failed to turn up in court. She had committed a number of property offences in the past which were related to her use of heroin and crack cocaine. She had a partner and a two-year old daughter who was being cared for by her mother-in-law. She had been a drug user for ten years and was on a methadone reduction programme. She had already spent a period of time in a residential rehabilitation unit but relapsed. Siobhan was found guilty by the courts and was given a probation order. Both her keyworker and her counsellor were involved in the process of securing a place for her in a residential rehabilitation unit. This was a difficult task because of the limited availability of appropriate treatment for women with children, in addition to the generic problems of long waiting lists and very limited community care funding. (Department of Health, 1996; SCODA, 1996).

Substance use

Siobhan was a heroin and crack cocaine user who had been involved with drugs from her late teens. Her involvement in crime, handling stolen goods, was directly related to her need to finance her dependence on drugs. The very decision to accept a current drug user like Siobhan into a hostel can be seen as a supportive measure as a deputy manager at Victoria House described.

> We would not refuse a woman because she was a drug user, which is not the case for all hostels. A lot of women who offend are drug users and we can't expect them to come to the hostel and be clean. We don't let them use on the premises but we will support them in the sense that they are not rejected by us.

The hostels studied were willing to take responsibility for women who use drugs. However, decisions to accept a drug user need to be made cautiously. When making decisions about referrals, hostel staff carefully considered the current balance of the hostel. Drug users were divided into the categories 'chaotic' and 'stable'. Those considered to be 'chaotic' were those still using illegal drugs, mainly heroin and cocaine, and who were not seeking to give up or reduce their drug use. Staff were cautious about accepting referrals from this group.

> If you know that somebody is a fairly chaotic drug user and on the referral it states that they will not seek counselling and you've got three others like that, then I will say no, but if someone is saying I will work on it and try to change . . . we will take them.
>
> (Manager, Carlton House)

The presence of individual drug users unwilling to seek help for their drug use in itself was not a problem, rather a concentration of 'chaotic' drug users was problematic, because it could potentially interfere with the smooth running of the hostel. At certain times, hostels could only accept those willing to work on their drug problem. Siobhan would not be characterised as 'chaotic'. She was willing to seek support for her drug dependence. Similarly Ruth was in contact with treatment services in relation to her drinking, and her drug use was largely 'recreational' drugs although she has experimented with a wide range of drugs in the past. Information on substance use would usually be known by the hostel at the referral stage. The next stage would be similar to that explained by an assistant manager at Victoria House.

116

Usually, if we start from the referral stage and the induction stage and we know that a woman has a drug or alcohol problem, we discuss it with the resident so they know that we are aware of these problems and if they wish to deal with it, we have the advice, we have the support and we will put that to them but it's up to them.

There would be an opportunity in keywork sessions to look at what they actually want to do and it would be sharing knowledge on resources available and what options they've actually got.

(Assistant manager, North Street Hostel)

This allows women, like Siobhan and Ruth, to consider the options open to them and to make choices about whether to try to give up and if so, how to give up. In this way, the women are given some control back over their own lives. It was made clear though to women like Siobhan and Ruth, and indeed all women, that using drugs within the hostel would result in being breached and returned to court. Siobhan's decision to seek support was made by herself with advice from hostel staff but her choice was a very constrained one. She was fearful of going into custody and fearful of losing her young daughter. For those like Siobhan who decide to give up their drug use, common to all hostels was the use of specialist drug agencies.

I suppose what we actually do is refer them to a counsellor and from the counselling sometimes they actually want more support from that. Through the keywork sessions you can actually highlight what support they are actually getting, what did it address and things like that.

(Assistant manager, Carlton House)

Use of external agencies can provide methadone prescriptions, if appropriate, and sometimes professional counselling to supplement the support a keyworker is able to give. The keyworker can offer additional help and advice or simply serve as someone to talk to. They are available on a regular basis within the constraints of the rota and the demands of other forms of hostel work. The additional support of her keyworker was welcomed by Siobhan because she appreciated the difficulties of giving up drug use, particularly in a residential setting. This can involve being surrounded by others who may be still using drugs, at an emotionally difficult and stressful time with the additional pressures she faced as the main carer of her young daughter.

Violence within relationships

Violence had been a central aspect of Heather's relationship with Charlie. The only respite she gained was during the periods in which he was in custody. The violence escalated to the point where her only survival strategy at the time appeared to be the use of force leading to his murder. This resulted in her first being remanded in custody and then referred to Victoria House. Heather was accepted by the hostel even though she was charged with a very serious, violent offence. Being charged with a violent offence or previous convictions for violence does not exclude an individual woman *per se.* Those likely to be excluded include those whose violent behaviour is likely to be directed at staff and residents in institutions or is likely to put the wider community at risk. Heather had committed a one off and highly specific act of violence aimed at one particular individual only. Thus she did not appear to present a risk to staff, other residents or the public.

Unusually, staff at Victoria House would be aware of Heather's experiences of violence before she arrived at the hostel. Typically, issues around violence and abuse would emerge later. Staff however tended to assume that most women referred to the hostel had experienced some form of emotional, physical or sexual abuse in the past, or were experiencing it now in an ongoing relationship. They were aware of women's vulnerability to violence, and in particular the vulnerability of the women who make up the hostel population.

> Violence is a big thing for a lot of the women.
>
> (Deputy manager, Carlton House)

> In women's hostels, you have to deal with the fact that the majority of residents have been abused throughout their lives.
>
> (Manager, Carlton House)

> I would say it was an issue that comes up time and time again for the women. Sometimes it doesn't come up but we would suspect it.
>
> (Assistant manager, North Street Hostel)

As the final comment illustrates, there are degrees to which residents are willing to talk about their experiences of violence and abuse. Some were not willing to discuss it whilst others would bring it to the attention of staff. However this latter group varied in the degree to which they require support.

> Sometimes people drop it into conversation and won't say more than that, and other times they will present it as a major issue that they want dealt with. It just depends how they bring it to you. Initially, you listen and then you take it from there.
>
> (Assistant manager, Victoria House)

It was seen as essential therefore to allow the woman to direct the extent to which she wanted to deal with the feelings and emotions that emerge from experiences of violence and abuse. For those who did not wish to discuss the matter further, their wishes were respected.

> We try to draw up an agenda for keyworking of what I and the resident want to talk about. Sometimes the things I want to talk about like . . . (abuse), she'll say 'I don't want to talk about' and you respect that and leave it alone. Hopefully, it will come up again. Sometimes it can be too painful to talk about just then.
>
> (Assistant manager, Victoria House)

However, there were instances where it was seen as necessary to approach the subject again; for example, if the effects of abuse manifested themselves in ways which were self-destructive and put the safety of the resident at risk (self-harm, eating disorders), or if violence was part of an ongoing relationship and visits from the partner to the hostel placed the safety of the particular resident, other residents and staff at risk. The deputy manager at Victoria House showed concern about the latter issue.

> If she's in an ongoing relationship and doesn't choose to do something about it then there is the question of whether we let the man into the hostel. If that violence occurs here, the staff have to deal with it so it's putting the woman at risk and the staff at risk.

In such a case hostel staff would take the initiative and refuse access to the partner involved. Problems tended to arise when a woman wanted a relationship to end but her partner kept visiting the hostel. There were instances of partners becoming abusive and making threats when a woman refused to see them. In these cases, staff expected women to take control over the situation as one of the assistant managers at Victoria House made clear, even if this went against the woman's wishes.

> If you've got a woman who says if my partner comes round, I don't want to see them because we've split up, you push it back to them and say you have to do this and we will support you. They are welcome to talk to their partner through the window and after that we pick it up so that the person isn't disturbed by it. Usually, it's not that clear cut. What usually happens is the scenario . . . with the woman that doesn't really want the relationship but at the same time if she goes through with it, she is left with nothing.

Other women made it explicit that they wanted the relationship to end and wanted to come to terms with what they had experienced, or wanted support around abusive experiences from the past. They hoped to use their period of residence in the hostel as an opportunity to explore their feelings and emotions stemming from their experiences.

Staff in the hostel did not engage in what they described as 'in-depth counselling'. Staff first listened to residents talk about their experiences but would ensure residents knew that additional help had to come from experts.

> I don't mind sitting listening to them but if they expect me to give anything back, I'm really not able to but I can give them information about where to go and follow that up with them.
>
> (Assistant manager, North Street Hostel)

However, access to counsellors was problematic, constrained by the high costs charged by professional counsellors and high levels of demand for counselling.

> In theory we have access to counsellors. In practice it is extremely difficult. It takes a number of phone calls. Calling on behalf of a resident recently I was told there was a three to four month waiting list. The reality and the theory often don't coincide.
>
> (Deputy manager, Carlton House)

What hostel staff were able to provide a back up to counselling. They could also offer the women an opportunity to talk about ways of managing and avoiding abusive situations, 'to let her know she doesn't need to take this kind of abuse' (Assistant manager, Victoria House). This would be approached in a non-directive way as described by the deputy manager at Victoria House.

> If a woman has come from a home environment where she's been battered and bruised by her partner, you can't say I think you should get out of it.

Encouraging women to challenge abuse is a difficult task given the widespread tolerance of abuse amongst women highlighted in the literature on domestic violence (Dobash and Dobash, 1998; Glass, 1995), and recognised by hostel staff.

> It's about undoing those beliefs that women have that it is OK to be abused, or it's right to be, that they deserve to be and what he says goes.
>
> (Deputy manager, Victoria House)

The same member of staff gave an example of one of the pressures women face who try to challenge abuse.

> For a lot of women, particularly around the acceptance of violence and abuse towards themselves, if they challenge it other residents may argue against it. So they are being quite firm with their partners who are coming and being abusive, but other residents are meddling their noses in and saying yeah but you shouldn't have said that. Basically they are saying he was in the right for behaving like that to you and you were wrong.

Pressures can be therefore be from within the relationship such as a partner who keeps telephoning or coming round, and externally from hostel residents, family and friends.

Heather was a good example of someone who tolerated her abuse, who tried to make excuses for the violent actions of her partner, Charlie, by blaming his alcohol abuse and the difficulty he had in controlling his temper. Her feelings whilst awaiting trial were of guilt and shame for retaliating with force, but also a realisation that she should have challenged the abuse previously and sought help from her family. She felt that she should not burden her family with her problems, but at the same time she did not feel she could talk to staff who in some ways were very much strangers.

121

Staff in all three hostels were aware of the difficulties women experienced in confiding in a member of the staff team.

> They don't always want to take part. It's very difficult for them to find someone to trust in a transient place.
>
> (Manager, Carlton House)

Time and energy therefore had to be invested into building up a relationship which allowed private issues to be highlighted, discussed and explored.

> We can give them time if they are here long enough . . . It's about establishing a relationship, respecting them as an individual, as grown up and giving them a chance to make decisions.
>
> (Assistant manager, Victoria House)

> I would say that if a woman was here for a long period of time, trust would be built up and they could talk about it (abuse) but for a lot of women it's very difficult.
>
> (Assistant manager, North Street Hostel)

It would be the role of Heather's keyworker then to make it known that she was available to talk whenever Heather felt she wanted to talk. In the meantime, keywork sessions could be spent establishing rapport, even through a informal conversation.

Offending behaviour

The stories of Siobhan, Heather, Judith and Ruth have in common experiences of being charged with a criminal offence. Reflected within their stories are very different patterns of offending. Siobhan had turned to property crime to support her drug use when her other sources of income had run out. Heather's violent attack leading to the death of her partner appears to have been very much an isolated incident. Judith suggested that her use of drugs 'sent her head funny' and as she could not think straight she began to get into trouble. She also noted that heavy drinking tended to make her aggressive. Ruth felt that her involvement in crime was related to the fact that all her family are involved in crime and that she always hangs about with the 'wrong people'. Using Stewart et al's (1994) typology, offending by Siobhan, Judith and Ruth could be characterised as lifestyle, where offending is intimately bound up with other aspects of an individual's life such as drug or alcohol use. Offending by Heather, Judith and Ruth could be viewed as self-expression, a reaction to stress, frustration and poor mental health, and Ruth's could also be seen as social activity, influenced by peer group pressures.

As unconvicted defendants, working on their offending behaviour was regarded by staff as optional, although explicitly encouraged. For example, Heather was reluctant to talk about her offence but staff continued to encourage her to speak to them when she felt able to.

> When they are on straight bail it can be difficult to maintain because they think I'm on bail, I'm not guilty, why am I doing this. Once they've actually been convicted and given a probation order to reside, we can move forward and actually look at those needs if they agree to look at those needs. That's how you can move forward but bailees are very different.
>
> (Deputy manager, Carlton House)

> People on probation, they've agreed to do the work and I do the work on their offending behaviour with them. People on bail, you cannot force them to do anything, you need their permission.
>
> (Deputy manager, North Street Hostel)

Different approaches were therefore required to cater for the needs of particular groups in a hybrid bail and probation hostel. In *National Standards for the Supervision of Offenders in the Community* (Home Office, 1995) different requirements for supervision are outlined for those on bail and those on probation. The principal difference stated is that those on probation should be involved in a programme[4] for their duration of their period of residence. However the rest of the guidance tries to provide generic guidance, and can be interpreted as lacking in realisation of the needs of particular categories of people within hostel and the practicalities of working with them.[5]

Offending behaviour was challenged and dealt with but in a more indirect way. For example, Siobhan's offending behaviour was tackled by working on her drug use, in the hope that this would lead to her no longer needing to offend.

> You do talk about the offending behaviour. I'm not saying you sit down and say tell me why you offended. You generally start by talking about the problems: sexual abuse, violence in the home, drug use perhaps as to why people continually steal or burgle; why a woman has killed or attempted to kill her partner. Maybe she's been beaten up over a certain number of years. You discuss offences but until you can get rid of the problems, violent partner, whatever, homelessness, they can't even begin to stop offending. It's a vicious circle.
>
> (Deputy manager, Victoria House)

> Theft, continuous drug-related theft and deception charges that people are on, in a roundabout way by working on their drug use you are also addressing that offending. It's not like you sit down and part of a keyworking session is recognising offending behaviour in its little compartment.
>
> (Manager, Victoria House)

Working with women on an everyday basis, supplemented by formal keyworking sessions.

> In a bail hostel . . . we see examples of behaviour which is very much linked with that offence . . . We challenge that behaviour on an everyday basis which I think is very effectual. You come back to somebody a week after they've done something and it's very difficult to sit back and recall the situation, but if you are able to challenge that behaviour . . . they are able to recognise it and link it in with the offence. You try to get them to recognise the link . . . I think that's one of the advantages of a hostel. You are able to address things on a day to day basis.
>
> (Deputy manager, Victoria House)

Therefore, work around offending behaviour took place but in a less formalised way than in other criminal justice agencies, for example the 'pathfinder'[6] programmes currently operating in probation services across England and Wales which should shortly be extended to approved hostels. An assistant manager at Victoria House who had previously worked in a prison drew out some comparisons.

When I worked in a prison we did a lot of work on offending behaviour, drawing life maps and tracing it back to see what triggered off their offending. You couldn't do it here. A lot of the women are so chaotic anyway that you wouldn't make much progress. It depends on the woman and how susceptible they are to looking at offending behaviour and if they want to change or not.

This member of staff highlighted some of the difficulties of working with this particular client group, in particular, the likelihood of a resident being prepared to work with a hostel worker in this way. More optimistically, one of her colleagues felt that more women were motivated to change.

I can't speak for my colleagues but we try as much as possible to bring offending behaviour into the foreground. Often the majority of residents will look at it. It's very rare that they are negative and won't look at it but the majority of the time it is taken on board by the resident.

The common ground shared by these workers is that women will vary in their willingness to work on their offending and therefore work in this area needs to be client-led. What staff can do is draw out the impact of their offending behaviour on their own lives and the lives of others such as their family, friends or victims. For those who demonstrate a desire to give up offending, staff can provide support. Initially, this entails working with women and listening to how they perceive their offending.

I think it helps to look at the circumstances of their lives and to look for patterns of offending. I see this with drug users when they have been using drugs, there are lots of offences and when they've been off it, its stopped. So we get them to look at that, the situation they were in at the time, how come it happened. That way you get them to look at it from a distance and to see how it affected them, the reasons why they did what they did and how they could avoid that sort of thing in the future.

(Deputy manager, Victoria House)

Keyworking is part of it. It's an important part to look at why women think they've offended and what are the issues that arise from it.

(Assistant manager, Victoria House)

125

They could then go on to provide specific support, both practical and emotional, around the issues involved directly or indirectly, drawing on the expertise of professionals where appropriate.

However, staff in all three hostels identified constraints in their work with women who wanted to adopt a law-abiding lifestyle. These included time, resources and adequacy of training. Time impacted on their work with women in the sense that women were often only residing in the hostel for a short period of time, and often they presented a number of issues which needed to be prioritised. For example, women sometimes presented issues which needed to be tackled immediately such as self-harm and eating disorders, in addition to their offending behaviour. Resources impacted on the provision of the service too, in particular the lack of funding to undertake groupwork. The difficulty hostels face in providing groupwork was further compounded by the lack of training amongst the staff team. In all three hostels, the only members of staff with a probation qualification were in managerial roles with heavy workloads and responsibilities. Other members of staff felt they lacked the prerequisite experience and qualifications to undertake this form of work as an assistant manager at North Street Hostel suggests.

> I need some training to talk to people how to tackle their offending, that's what I need to know and I know that's what I need . . . I don't feel confident enough to challenge people in their offending. I don't think it is fair to the people that I'm working with that I enter into something like that where I don't know what I'm talking about . . . It could be a bit explosive almost. I could do some damage really. It's not fair on me either.

Hostels worked within these constraints to provide what could be loosely termed offending behaviour programmes. At Victoria House, residents were encouraged to make use of voluntary projects. At Carlton House, residents were offered short sessions and linked in with local probation facilities where possible, and at North Street Hostel, offending behaviour sessions were linked into a wider life skills group programme.

Is this a feminist approach?

Drawing upon different feminist traditions (liberal, radical and postmodern) and different social work perspectives (both traditional and radical), a feminist critique of current social work practice has developed. Work by feminists such as Buckley and Wilson (1989), Dominelli and McLeod (1989), Hanmer and Statham (1988), Langan and Day (1992) and Wright and Kemshall (1994) has delineated a number of crucial aspects of a woman-centred approach. These include a focus on structural explanations and recognition of the gendered nature of oppression; recognition of the commonality of experience between female clients and female workers but also a realisation of the heterogeneity of experience amongst women divided by class, race and sexuality; a focus on empowerment and an emphasis on valuing women through self-determination such that the client directs the social work relationship. Langan (1992, pp.1-2) argues that:

> the new approach recognises the complexity and diversity of the manifold oppressions that affect the lives of most women and most social work clients.

The approach adopted by staff has some parallels with the characteristics of the approach outlined by feminist social workers. However, staff did not explicitly use the term feminist and may have actively rejected the use of the term. Their emphasis was very much on a client-centred approach, compatible with feminist social work. There were other areas of compatibility. For example, they highlighted differences between women.

> We get a mix of people.
>
> (Assistant manager, Carlton House)

> Because you are here it doesn't mean you have to have keyworking sessions. If the woman refuses which happens quite often, particularly with black residents, they are very independent.
>
> (Assistant manager, Victoria House)

However, they also strongly stressed commonality. For instance:

127

A lot of the women by the time they've got here are in crisis.

(Deputy manager, Victoria House)

The majority I would say are in crisis, a high proportion are damaged.

(Night support worker, Victoria House)

However, there were some notable areas of discrepancy beyond that which emerges when theoretical ideas are translated into practical contexts. In particular, there were few references to commonality between worker and client. In some ways, they saw themselves as more fortunate and privileged, as in control of their own lives in contrast to their female clients, often described as in crisis.

I think often for people, apart from their background, another situation they are stuck in is having very little money and all the things that say are available to me as a working woman, to take advantage of like going to leisure centres, the pictures . . . That's the sort of the thing people who come into the hostel haven't got the opportunities to do.

(Deputy manager, Victoria House)

Whilst the issues that women present may touch on those which have affected their own lives, the differences between workers and clients were discussed more than similarities. This along with their role as workers in an approved hostel to supervise and enforce discipline created power differentials which mitigated against the establishment of a non-hierarchical relationship stressed in some feminist social work literature (Hanmer and Statham, 1988; Wright and Kemshall, 1994). The function of the bail and probation hostel as a criminal justice institution was therefore crucial.

Strong arguments have also been made for the adoption of feminist or 'womanwise' (Carlen, 1998) approach to work with female offenders. Over the past three decades many feminist criminologists and pressure groups have argued that women are treated unfavourably in the prison system (for example, Carlen, 1990 and 1998; Eaton, 1993). Carlen and members of Women in Prison, a pressure group concerned exclusively with women who appear before the courts, have argued that this can be usefully summarised in the slogan 'discipline, infantalize, feminize, medicalize and

128

domesticize' (Carlen, 1985, p.182). There has been some recognition by the Prison Service that changes need to be made to the way women prisoners are treated but recent documents, principally the Thematic Review (HM Inspectorate of Prisons, 1997) have tended to concentrate on a wide range of pertinent issues such as appropriate security, retaining family ties, health care and sentence planning but have had little to say about the principles which guide day-to-day work with women. On this particular issue *Regimes for Women* published by the Prison Service in 1992 was a step in the right direction. The document sketched a regime with the key elements to encourage, to support, to listen, to help, to provide, to enable, to recognise and to care. The extent to which this theoretical model can actually be translated in day-to-day work with women is questionable, and thus many feminist criminologists (particularly Pat Carlen), pressure groups and indeed the hostel workers interviewed for this study advocated greater use of community penalties, including the use of probation hostels.

Some comparisons between working with women and men

It is commonly argued that women and men who appear before the courts have different problems and thus different support needs. We have already explored in this chapter the key issues presented by women. Those who worked with men suggested that the key issues presented by men included offending, substance use, mental health problems, experiences of abuse and family and relationship problems. A recent literature reviewed prepared for HM Prison Service found that many of the criminogenic factors associated with male offenders are relevant to female offenders but their level of importance and the nature of the association may differ (Howden-Windell and Clark, 1999). This small-scale study found evidence that whilst women and men often experience similar problems, there are some important differences as well. Practitioners, policy-makers and academics therefore need to recognise, but not exaggerate, the similarities between women and men who offend. However, the same groups need also to be alert to areas of divergence.

In the mixed hostel, staff argued that women and men tended to commit different types of offences, and for different reasons.

The reasons why women are here are often very different from why the men are here . . . It's very rare that you would get a woman who is on charges of taking cars. In my experience they are more things to do with drug use, or their own safety. We don't get many on burglary charges.

(Assistant manager, North Street Hostel)

There are very different reasons why women offend and why men offend and that's reflected in the different types of offences that are committed . . . For the women who come here it's largely to do with drugs – deception, shoplifting, theft. We sometimes get a violent offence but not very often. Whereas with the male population it would be a wide range of issues – lots of car crime, burglary, theft.

(Deputy manager, North Street Hostel)

There were other key differences as well. Whilst it was recognised that some men had experiences of violent and abusive relationships, it was seen as more prevalent amongst female residents. Male residents were perceived as more likely to be homeless and to be alcohol dependent. They were also judged as less likely to experience problems in finding people to care for their children. However whilst staff were able to articulate gender differences, workers were keen to avoid essentialist arguments. For example:

Within their group they [women] are diverse and so are the men here very diverse within their group but there are certainly more differences, I would say, between the two groups rather than within the two groups.

(Assistant manager, North Street Hostel)

Working with women and men in a mixed setting

Recognising the different needs of female and male prisoners. Carlen (1998) argues for different regimes which can be justified in the basis of 'ameliorative justice', a principle that assumes that women are more likely to suffer the pains of imprisonment. She suggest that this needs to be combined with 'gender-testing'; in other words, a testing of all new regime initiatives and security innovations to assess whether or not the implementation of new measures would disproportionately worsen the situation of either women or men. There are some difficulties in applying this approach to hostels where women comprise the minority of the resident population.

In mixed hostels, equality of opportunity is difficult to achieve as the accounts of hostel workers make clear. It may lead to direct discrimination, but a more likely outcome is indirect discrimination whereby the needs of female residents get overlooked. This was one reservation shared by many of the staff in women-only hostels.

> You taken any mixed environment, men and women; mainly men get
> the first slice of the cake.
>
> (Assistant manager, Victoria House)

> In mixed hostels there should be greater care to ensure that women
> aren't undermined, undervalued or treated differently.
>
> (Deputy manager, Victoria House)

Within women-only hostels, staff are available to develop a specialist service. For example, both women-only hostels had developed links with specialist agencies which catered for the problems experienced by female residents and provided activities which aimed to increase women's self-esteem. However, within the mixed hostel, staff were trying to reconcile a realisation of the different needs of female and male residents with practical realities. The key practical issues included: the problem of scarce resources (principally competing demands on staff time) and the problem of working with a small and fluctuating female population. The mixed hostel had four beds reserved for women at all times, despite the knock-on effect on the occupancy rates when these beds were not filled.[7] However, as mentioned previously, rarely were all the women's beds in use. As a result, the development of the groupwork programme, for example, was driven by the needs of male residents. As a result, it focused largely on crimes more likely to be committed by men such as burglary or car crime, and challenging behaviour associated with masculinity such as aggression. The particular needs of female residents which may include strategies for dealing with violence or assertiveness were therefore glossed over. Instead, support for female residents largely took the form of referral to outside agencies, but staff felt that much work needed to be done on building up a portfolio of ways in which women could be supported. Two assistant managers at North Street Hostel reflected on some of the limitations of existing practice.

> It's a shame because I'm sure they feel they don't get enough
> support and to a certain extent they probably don't get enough of the

support they want . . . Women need different support to men often and I don't think that is necessarily taken into account.

I think someone needs to spend a lot of time thinking about what we offer women . . . I think someone needs to be looking at the groupwork programme and linking the women up with probation groups. We owe it to the women . . . I can't see it happening.

Some steps had been taken to avoid discrimination against women in a largely male environment. For example, women were provided with televisions in their rooms, were not obliged to attend meetings or group sessions and were allowed to self-cater. The measures were founded on a realisation of the fact that women may feel intimidated in a room full of male residents, particularly if they had suffered abuse from men in the past. However, this did lead to friction, as an assistant manager at North Street Hostel described:

Every so often, there is a rise of resentment because the women are treated differently and, try as you might to explain to people why it is only fair to treat some people differently in order to be fair, they don't grasp it. It is a difficult concept to grasp, especially if you are not happy with how you are being treated.

What is acknowledged here is that working with both women and men in mixed hostels is not a straightforward issue. In order to ensure equality of opportunity, consideration has to be given to overcoming the possible sources of disadvantage women may face in such a setting. The situation is more complex than ensuring all individuals are treated exactly the same but this can be a difficult concept to put into practice.

Concluding comments

In this chapter we have explored the principles which guide residential work with women. We also examined some of the difficulties encountered when these principles are applied to real-life situations. As others have argued, inevitably the professional ideologies which inform practice are 'mediated by the exigencies of practice' (Hardiker, 1977, p.153) and the power of the agency function (Wright and Kemshall, 1994, p.77), in this instance a criminal justice institution. The example of working with women in a mixed setting where they comprise the minority of clients provides one vivid illustration of the difficulties of putting professional ideologies of working with women into practice when faced with difficulties such as inadequate resources. In the next chapter we explore the realities of everyday life in hostels further, and consider the key factors which contribute to the success or otherwise of working with offenders in residential settings.

Notes

1. The women-only hostels only employed women (see chapter two). The mixed hostel did employ male staff but none of these agreed to be interviewed. There was no deliberate policy to exclude male staff and interviews were conducted with five men working in a male-only hostel.

2. These issues are explored in Wincup, 1998; 1999a and 2000.

3. I subsequently discovered through media reports that she received a short custodial sentence.

4. The term 'programme' is not defined but is assumed to mean an individualised programme designed to address their offending behaviour and welfare needs.

5. As we discussed in chapter three, the 2000 version does not make the distinction between bailees and those on probation.

6. Pathfinder projects are pilot projects which are being developed to determine 'what works' (see chapter eight) with offenders on community penalties. They are being developed for hostels to test different regimes.

7. This is significant because the only Key Performance Indicator for hostels is occupancy.

8 Evaluating Residential Work with Offenders

Introduction

Previous chapters have explored the difficulties faced by residential workers in carrying out their day-to-day work with offenders. Having recognised these difficulties, we might ask why people continue with such work? In part this can be answered by recognising that residential work with offenders offers challenging opportunities which can be viewed positively as a source of job satisfaction, as well as a source of stress. Job satisfaction derives from many sources but particularly from hostel workers' ability to recognise that their work is successful. This chapter provides an analysis of hostel workers' definitions of success, and delineates the factors which facilitate or impinge upon their work with offenders. This is set against a backdrop of increasing pressures on the Probation Service to evaluate its practice.

From 'nothing works' to effective practice: A potted history

Over the past two decades, pressures on the Probation Service to improve and demonstrate effectiveness have been intense. Such pressures are not peculiar to the Probation Service. Rather they have been felt sharply by other criminal justice agencies including the courts, the Prison Service and the Police (McLaughlin and Muncie, 1994), and indeed many other public sector organisations, particularly health (Walby and Greenwell, 1994) and education (Fergusson, 1994). Organisations have been forced to justify their existence and re-imagine themselves in terms of quasi-market competitiveness, core competencies, rigorous resource control, customer responsiveness, quality of service and certifiable cost-effectiveness (McLaughlin and Muncie, 1996). This form of 'new managerialism' (May, 1991) prioritises bureaucratisation, performance measurement and administrative control, advancing the role of status of management at the expense of professionals.

In a recent guide to effective practice published by HM Inspectorate of Probation, Chapman and Hough (1998) outlined a number of features in the development of recent probation policy which have created pressures to improve and demonstrate effectiveness. As we discussed earlier in chapter two, the Probation Service has witnessed many significant changes over the last three decades, From its earliest origins towards the end of the 19th century to the beginning of the 1970s, the Probation Service strictly adhered to a rehabilitative or social work ethos, targeting its efforts on less serious offenders in order to prevent them from future harm. A major challenge to this approach took place in the mid-1970s as a consequence of political and academic challenges. Worrall (1997a) refers to these as 'libertarian', 'New Right' and 'pragmatic' challenges. The former suggested that treatment disguised state control and argued that civil liberties were being infringed as people were being 'treated' for periods of time disproportionate to the offence committed. In contrast, the ideology of the New Right sought greater control over offenders and emphasised the need for greater surveillance. Of particular relevance to debate about effectiveness is the pragmatist challenge. Pragmatists highlighted the perceived ineffectiveness of criminal justice interventions by drawing upon the findings of a series of well-resourced experimental and quasi-experimental studies (Folkard et al, 1976, Phillpots and Lancucki, 1979). Together these studies appeared to demonstrate that rehabilitation programmes were 'at best . . . a waste of energy and commitment, and at worst . . . counterproductive' (Raynor and Vanstone, 1994; p.398). The most influential was the one conducted by Martinson (1974) which was widely interpreted as 'nothing works'. This 'nothing works' pessimism undermined the professional self-confidence of the service. However, as Chapman and Hough (1998) noted, this challenge took place at a time when probation services had considerable local autonomy and resources were not under threat. Consequently, there was no immediate pressure to improve or demonstrate effectiveness but there was a fundamental shift in probation practice away from 'treatment' towards 'help', informed choice, diversion and crime prevention (Shaw 1996). The Probation Service was no longer sure of its foundation and the issue of 'care versus control' came to dominate professional thinking in the early 1980s (Worrall 1997a).

Reversing in part the tendency to assume 'nothing works', political and academic opinion altered and in the 1980s a common view was that any sentencing intervention had a marginal impact on offending. The realisation that costly prison sentences had no greater deterrent or rehabilitative effect than community penalties paved the way for the growth of community penalties to divert offenders from custody. This expansion was accompanied by gradual exposure to public sector managerialism beginning in 1984 with the publication of a *Statement of National Objectives and Priorities*. In the early 1990s, budgetary expansion was replaced by cash limited budgets. Probation services found themselves subject to rising case loads at the same time as they were subjected to initiatives which purported to improve efficiency and effectiveness (Humphrey and Pease, 1992). The seeming incapability or unwillingness of the Probation Service and other criminal justice agencies to respond to increasing criticism and put their own house in order persuaded the Conservative Government to open up the criminal justice system to the watchful eye of auditors and management consultants (McLaughlin and Muncie, 1994). These professional groups were happier dealing with costing issues rather than service quality, which they preferred to leave to the Probation Service and research conducted at the time demonstrates the dissatisfaction of probation officers with this statistical approach (Humphrey and Pease, 1992). Evaluation took place in a rudimentary form and could more accurately be characterised as monitoring of the inputs and outputs of probation practice. Reconviction rates were emphasised as a measure of success despite their well-documented limitations (Brownlee, 1998; Chapman and Hough, 1998; Lloyd et al, 1994, Raynor and Vanstone, 1994).

Managerialism still prevails but it is no longer accompanied by the pessimism of 'nothing works'. As Pitts (1992) notes the 'nothing works' doctrine has been replaced with a 'something works' doctrine. Researchers have reached a more limited but undoubtedly more realistic conclusion that rehabilitative interventions can work under closely defined circumstances if accurately targeted and correctly implemented. In other words we have witnessed a growing acceptance that something or somethings work for some people some of the time (Worrall, 1997a).

This new mood of optimism paved the way for a revival of interest in treatment methods, particularly cognitive-behavioural approaches and encouraged gradual rethinking of the non-treatment paradigm. Researchers have begun to ask what works (McGuire, 1995; Vennard et al, 1997) and have synthesised existing research findings, in addition to drawing on evidence from new research. Added on to the question 'what works?' are two important points of clarification: for whom and under what conditions? Evaluation research needs to translate into evidence-based practice and the task of the Probation Service is to ensure that the existing knowledge based about effective practice is applied, to extend the knowledge base and to develop management systems for maximising effectiveness (Chapman and Hough, 1998). However, the answer to the question 'what works?' is in some respects pre-determined (Mair, 2000; Morgan, 2000) and is danger of being seen as 'the solution' (Worrall, 1997a, p.117, emphasis in original). As Hannah-Moffat and Shaw (2000, p.9) suggest 'it is important to temper the current rush to see cognitive skills as the answer to the probation officer's prayer'. Cognitive behavioural techniques have been prioritised which require the active participation of the offender in programmes which are proportionate to the actuarial assessment of risk. These programmes are to be carefully targeted, strictly enforced and rigorously evaluated. Whilst this orthodoxy about what constitutes effective probation practice may prevail, the need to improve and demonstrate effectiveness is now central to the work of Probation Service.

Effectiveness has now been broadly defined by HM Inspectorate of Probation (Underdown, 1998) as the 'reduction/cessation of offending; completion of the order to national standards; development of positive attitudes and behaviour; improvement in factors linked to offending (criminogenic needs) and improvement in social circumstances/community integration'. A national implementation strategy (known as the Effective Practice Initiative) was devised and issued in Probation Circular 35/98. Pathfinder programmes funded under the Crime Reduction Programme and Effective Practice Initiative are required to evaluate the impact of extra spending on levels of crime (Colledge, et al, 1999). The new emphasis on effective practice has the potential to transform work with offenders and to promote the development of professional skills. It provides an opportunity for real evaluation of the work done with offender to supplement the collection of data on Key Performance Indicators At the same time the bottom line is that local probation services will be unable to justify their public funding and their existence without evidence of effective practice.

Assessing the impact on bail and probation hostels

Pressures to improve and demonstrate effectiveness have had far-reaching implications of bail and probation hostels, especially with regard to the introduction of Key Performance Indicators (KPIs). At the time the research was conducted, the Home Office had set two KPIs and related targets specifically related to bail/probation hostels. These were introduced in 1994 following the publication of the rolling three year plan for the Probation Service. These were to measure the number of occupied bed spaces in approved hostels against the number of bed spaces available and the proportion of hostel residents completing orders. Following the review of KPIs for the service, the latter has now been designated a 'Supporting Management Information Need' (HM Inspectorate of Probation, 1998). Consequently, the only national specific indicator for hostel performance relates to occupancy. Whilst this is an important measure, as HM Inspectors noted in their 1998 report, consideration needs to be given to establishment of agreed or additional KPIs to enable comparative performance to be assessed.

The introduction of these KPIs appears to have had a dramatic effect. The average level of occupancy has increased from 68 percent in 1993 to 85 percent in 1997, exceeding the Home Office target of 83 percent (for 1997-98). However, a careful reading of these statistics is needed. There has been a slow but significant reduction during the 1990s in both the number of hostels within the approved sector as well as in their bed capacity. In part this is due to unsuitability but other closures have occurred because of a failure to achieve satisfactory occupancy rates. It has been brought home sharply to hostel managers the implications of failing to meet Home Office targets. Consequently, as previously discussed in chapter five, the emphasis on measuring occupancy was a source of anxiety for hostel managers. Hostel workers' perceptions of the value of KPIs are explored later in this chapter.

Beyond these KPIs there are few formal mechanisms in hostels for evaluating the impact of the hostel on resident's attitudes or likely future behaviour although a handbook for hostels designed to assist in the delivery of cost-effective residential facilities was issued in October 1995. There appears scope for future sustained development along the lines suggested in the HM Inspectorate of Probation (1998) report on the work of approved probation and bail hostels; a national initiative to provide a framework for all hostels to begin to assess the impact of the hostel on residents.

Some probation services have used resident questionnaires in order to evaluate the service from the consumers' point of view covering topics such as induction, keyworking, and anti-discriminatory practice; as well as inviting general comments about each resident's stay at an approved hostel. This method was used at Victoria House to obtain feedback from residents. The HM Inspectorate of Probation (1998) report notes that five of the seventeen hostels inspected had introduced feedback forms but there was little evidence of the collated results being actively used to improve practice. An exercise such as conducting a survey amongst residents has a number of strengths because clients are silenced in the current 'what works?' discourse (Beaumont and Mistry, 1996). Client feedback is of particular relevance to process evaluations (Chapman and Hough, 1998). Other researchers have warned of the dangers of placing too much emphasis on simple 'satisfaction' ratings and argue that at the very least generalities must be disaggregated, and the context from which individuals are evaluating their experiences must be explored (Cheetham et al, 1992).

The implications of the current emphasis on evidence-based practice for bail and probation hostels are unclear. There are copious references in the Chapman and Hough (1998) volume to systematic interventions and planned programmes of work. Programmes are broadly defined to refer to a planned series of interventions over a specified and bounded period of time which can be demonstrated to positively change attitudes, beliefs, behaviour and social circumstances. Chapman and Hough focused their guide on the supervision of offenders on probation, community service and combination orders but note that there is scope to apply the basic principles of effective practice to all areas of probation practice. Whilst these principles can be related directly to some work in hostels such as keyworking with those on probation or groupwork programmes, it is more difficult to apply them to work with bailees who are resident in hostels for a short and/or undefined amount of time. The lack of training for hostel workers in general (see chapter four), and on evaluation in particular, is a further obstacle. Lack of training on evaluation is shared with colleagues throughout the Probation Service. Whilst such skills are incorporated into the new probation curriculum, the first cohort of trainee probation officers only just completed their training. Probation services are struggling to cope with the demands of the new focus on effective training and are seeking training in the form of short courses from universities. Other barriers to evaluating practice included insufficient staff and computer resources (Donohoe, 2000). Donohoe argues that 'we need efficient systems and committed supportive staff and managers to enable full development of an evidence based practice agenda' (p.34). In order to achieve this, more constructive steps at ground level are needed to empower officers to evaluate practice, and subsequently provide evidence.

Effectiveness and hostel work: Professional accounts

The remainder of the chapter draws on narrative accounts by hostel workers, in order to identify their evaluating strategies and the evidences they draw on to decide whether or not their work has gone well. It begins with a critical discussion of official measures of success.

Official measures: A critique

Hostel staff expressed considerable concerns about what they perceived as an over reliance on KPIs. One of the limitations of quantitative outcome measures such as KPIs is their failure to appreciate the practicalities of service delivery. Staff continually emphasised that these needed to be comprehended to understand the processes which influence occupancy rates or completed periods of residence. There views have many parallels with Short (1980).

> Primary attention to measuring final outcomes or 'impact' can, in the extreme, lead to so called 'black-box' evaluation where the content and process of service delivery are left completely unexamined.
> (Short, 1980; cited in Loseke, 1989, pp.202-203)

Staff argued that occupancy rates cannot always be interpreted as indicative of unsatisfactory hostel performance. For example, low occupancy rates may be the result of a lack of referrals, an increase in the use of custodial demands or a loss of beds due to a refurbishment programme. High occupancy rates may reflect a willingness to accept individuals for whom a hostel placement is not appropriate because they present a risk to staff, residents and the public or because their offence is minor and their main need is accommodation. Similarly, the limitations of occupancy rates have been discussed elsewhere.

> Although the occupancy rate is a useful performance indicator for hostels, as with other performance indicators in general, it should be understood as a means to an end and not an end in itself . . . An occupancy rate on its own cannot provide an unequivocal measure of a hostel.
>
> (Lewis and Mair, 1989, p.9)

Reactions to the monitoring of successful completions were mixed. A number of hostel workers pointed out that for many residents simply staying at the hostel was an important achievement in itself. They described the multiple and complex problems residents were experiencing in addition to their offending and the fact that many of them had previously broken bail in the past (Wincup, 1999a; see also Lewis and Mair, 1989).

> I think if they manage to stay here successfully during the bail period that's the most important thing.
>
> (Assistant manager, North Street Hostel)

> I think if they go through their bail period that's achieving an awful lot. I would say that if somebody successfully completed their bail period without being breached that is good.
>
> (Assistant manager, North Street Hostel)

The main concern of staff related to the ways in which completion rates were interpreted. Staff emphasised that unsuccessful completions, usually due to either the resident absconding or being breached, should not be regarded as failure on behalf of the hostel.

> If women abscond, it doesn't mean they don't like the hostel. They may abscond because they are scared a partner knows where they are, or are scared about the court proceedings or have reoffended . . . There a number of reasons why women abscond. It's not so clear cut as they don't like the hostel.
>
> (Assistant manager, Victoria House)

> Successful completions is obviously a target the Home Office has selected. However, people do tend to get breached because of their behaviour.
>
> (Assistant manager, Carlton House)

141

In the latter case, it could be argued that breaching a resident demonstrates successful working on behalf of the hostel because hostels are required to strictly enforce the orders of the court, *National Standards* and hostel rules. Low numbers of completed periods of residence may be the consequence of hostels being willing to take very high risk individuals or because hostels are alert to breaches of hostel rules. Conversely, a high percentage of completed periods of residence may be the consequence of staff being unwilling to breach residents even when hostel rules have been broken.

The consensus was that success could not be measured through the narrowly defined KPIs used by the Home Office. Instead, staff emphasised the multi-faceted nature of success in relation to residential work with offenders.

> It depends on how you look at it. There are all different kinds of success isn't there.
>
> (Assistant manager, North Street Hostel)

> I don't know how you measure that really. You could say that success is someone who goes through that door and never offends again. It could be many things. If someone lessens their drug use . . .
> if they reduce the seriousness of their offending, if their self-esteem and their ability to cope develops. Some of those things to some degree can be seen as success.
>
> (Deputy manager, Carlton House)

Defining success: Hostel workers' accounts

Although there were varying views on what constituted successful residential work with offenders, a common theme was the adherence to more subjective and personalised ways of measuring success when compared to Home Office KPIs. For staff, their emphasis was on whether individual residents had made any changes to their lives.

> Our measure of success is whether there has been a change, a positive change in someone's life.
>
> (Deputy manager, Harding House)

> For the women, its getting them through their orders and seeing some sort of growth in them, in that they've got somewhere

142

compared to how they were when they came in. I think that's an important thing.

(Manager, Carlton House)

You haven't done any amazing thing but you may have helped to see what they are about.

(Assistant manager, Harding House)

I don't know whether you can change people but what you hope to do is change their perceptions of things slightly so that they begin to think of something else. If you've done that in a tiny way to say 10 percent of your throughput, I think you're doing OK.

(Assistant manager, Harding House)

As Humphrey and Pease (1992) note, the measurement of effectiveness is complex and ethereal in service organisations such as the Probation Service. Many of the hostel workers interviewed shared the view that concept of effectiveness is inherently nebulous.

I would say we have a measure of success in our face to face work with people but people are immeasurable things.

(Assistant manager, Harding House)

It's difficult in a job like this, If you are trying to convince lay people, people outside the criminal justice system, that what you are doing is worthwhile, how they hell do you judge that? You can only judge success or failure at a very individual level.

(Deputy manager, Harding House)

One of the problems of official measures is that success is not measured in relation to its impact on an individual and their particular needs. In recent years, there has been a great deal of time and energy devoted to developing instruments to measure attitudinal changes (e.g. the CRIME-PICS scale developed by Frude et al, 1994) and offender risk and criminogenic needs (e.g. LSI-R, ACE and OASys). Structured assessment tools have a number of strengths but they are not *the* solution to the problems of measuring the impact of residential work on offenders (see chapter two).

The most pervasive theme in staff accounts was the need for a realism. There was some resentment that the expectations of hostel work were too high.

143

Change people's lives. That's what we are supposed to do but you
know and I know that its just not like that.

(Assistant manager, Harding House)

You need to look at it realistically. For example, if a woman comes
in and reduces her offending to cheque book fraud occasionally that
is success. The ideal, or the official view is to give up offending
altogether.

(Assistant manager, Carlton House)

I would find the job very demoralising if I really expected people to
make massive progress while they were here. You need to be
realistic.

(Assistant manager, North Street Hostel)

However, staff did not hold the view that change was not possible. Instead,
they recognised that the process of change can be characterised as slow and
incremental and sometimes felt that it was like taking 'two steps forward
and one back'. Hostel workers placed great stress on the achievement of
small, incremental goals and were happy with steady step by step changes.
Grand goals tended be eschewed in favour of chipping away at problems.

Just doing simple things can be a success. If we can build on that so
much the better. Perhaps get them to stop offending, even if it's only
whilst they are here.

(Deputy manager, Harding House)

We probably won't have eradicated all their problems but we've
provided them with a safe environment and we've managed to help
them through a court appearance with some resolution at the end.
That's the success really.

(Assistant manager, Victoria House)

The emphasis on small, incremental steps was reflected in some of the
evidence they cited for quality of practice. Changes which may seem minor
to external observers were noted as a sign that hostel workers can make a
difference to people's lives.

If we can as a staff team offer accommodation to a chaotic drug user
who is at the point of not surviving, again that is a success. In other
people's eyes perhaps they're not doing anything fantastic but they

144

are eating, they've cut down a bit on their drug use and they are getting hold of clean needles not dirty ones. That's a bloody big success and if that's all we are doing we are doing our job. So yes I think we are quite successful.

(Deputy manager, Victoria House)

If you can get someone to wash and clean regularly when they didn't before that's a success.

(Assistant manager, Harding House)

You measure success in a very basic way. You have to measure it that way. OK they made it to an appointment. They caused a fuss when they got there. That's a success. The fact that we couldn't convince them that going to see their probation officer was a good idea falls by the wayside.

(Deputy manager, Victoria House)

Getting someone to say yeah that bloke hit me and he shouldn't have done. Even if I'd done that he shouldn't have hit me. If I can get one person to recognise that, that for me is a success.

(Deputy manager, Victoria House)

From hostel workers' accounts it becomes apparent that the process of change is a complex one. Change may not be evident at first in tangible way. Hostel workers' argued that during an offender's period of residence in a hostel the process of change can commence but is rarely completed.

It's about putting seeds into people's heads . . . I don't think we ever finish and my expectation is not to finish. We, I suppose, spark it off; just sort of set it up a it and for me that is success.

(Deputy manager, Victoria House)

Loseke's (1989) exploration of the meaning of success amongst workers on a family violence programme found similar views. One worker she interviewed commented:

I've reached the point . . . where I prefer to think of myself as a seed planter if nothing better . . . and it's comforting for me to think that if I haven't been able to solve this lady's problems . . . then at least I've been able to present her with the opportunity to tell her some of the facts about violence.

145

Using the imagery of a 'seed planter', success can only be apparent in retrospect, making it difficult to evaluate the degree of success. Again this contributes to the difficulty of measuring 'success' in relation to residential work with offenders.

> You would need to monitor it over a decade or so.
> (Assistant manager, Harding House)

> I have to keep in my mind that everybody is capable of change but
> it's a process that isn't going to happen overnight.
> (Night support worker, Victoria House)

> If you tell people something now they don't have to use it now and
> come 5, 10 or 15 years time they may remember it. That's enough
> for me.
> (Assistant manager, North Street Hostel)

One of the most commonly used evidences staff drew upon to demonstrate the potential of residential work with offenders were 'success stories' of ex-residents. These demonstrated that whilst the process of change was usually slow, incremental and sometimes not apparent, in some cases residents, particularly long-term ones, were able to make more dramatic changes. None of the hostels had formalised means of following up ex-residents but sometimes residents kept in contact with their keyworker. This was particular the case at Victoria House because move-on accommodation for ex-offenders was located close by.

> I can think of one woman who came to us with a heroin habit. The
> hostel had its input but it was a lot more than that. Through coming
> to the hostel and having an excellent keyworker . . . when she left,
> with the hostel reports given, she was able to escape a custodial
> sentence. She was then after a time given a place in a cluster house
> on its own with very limited support. We, over a period of time
> helped her through her probation order and that woman has been
> drug free for three years . . . That's a success story. Another success
> could be a woman on a murder charge linked to domestic violence.
> She was found guilty by the courts but her keyworker never left her
> and kept supporting her all the way through. She went for a retrial
> and she was found guilty of manslaughter and she'd served the
> sentence she was given already. The relationship was a continuing

146

one and that's a success story because of the support the woman got from the hostel.

(Night support worker, Victoria House)

The ideal, or the official view is to give up offending altogether. That does happen sometimes. For example, we had a woman come here who was a prostitute earning £200 a day and she gave it up and went to college to study, supplementing her grant with part-time work.

(Assistant manager, Carlton House)

Someone left recently who seemed like a real success to me. They had been going to anger management. They'd attended that and got quite a lot out of that, and in general had just stabilised. They had progressed and moved on. They had used up most of what we were offering and fitted in to our ideas about how things are supposed to work. They were a model resident in my eyes.

(Assistant manager, North Street Hostel)

Just as evidence from ex-residents could be used to demonstrate effective practice, equally it could be used to demonstrate seemingly ineffective practice as one worker commented.

Why do we see the same people come back to us time after time?

(Deputy manager, Harding House)

What determines success?

This section explores some of the factors which hostel workers believe need to be in place if work is to have a chance of going well. There is an important caveat in the success story recounted by one of the night support workers at Victoria House above. Whilst acknowledging the input of the hostel, she commented 'but it was a lot more than that'. Success seems to depend on many factors. These factors can be used as mitigating factors if work does not go well, therefore 'protecting' the hostel staff team and forming part of an 'occupational survival kit (Bull and Shaw, 1992, p.643). It would be unfair to say that hostel workers duck out of all responsibility. As we will explore later in this chapter, hostel workers frequently set themselves high, perhaps unrealistic, standards and have to learn to

147

manage their feelings in the face of perceived failure. Let us explore now these factors in turn.

1   Individual factors

> You can't win them all.
>
> (Night support worker, Harding House)

The comment from the night support worker above epitomises one of the key themes in the hostel workers' accounts. They constantly expressed the view that success is not inevitable and was contingent on a number of factors relating to an individual residents: the circumstance of their lives, their motivation to change and their ability to seek help and support. Let us discuss these factors in turn.

The residents they were working with often had multiple and complex problems (Lewis and Mair, 1989; Wincup, 1999a). Offending behaviour was often combined with a wide range of other issues such as substance use, relationship problems, poor physical and mental health and homelessness. Consequently, staff had to prioritise their work with such residents and deal with immediate issues first, for example linking a drug user in with the community drugs team.

> Life is totally upside down when they come here and I see it as our job to get the basics worked in and then let people know what is available so they can move on to take up that support.
>
> (Deputy manager, Victoria House)

Sometimes residents were able to move on to take up other forms of support available but other times this was not possible as an assistant manager at Victoria House explained.

> It's a heavy thing to be on a serious criminal charge and beside that there may be other things going on like a drug-related problem. It's difficult for the women to see those things we have on offer.
>
> (Assistant manager, Victoria House)

In some instance, residents were aware of the support on offer but were reluctant to change their lives. Hostel staff shared the view that residents needed to be motivated in order for the process of change to be successful and permanent.

148

You might set up a place in a rehab. [residential drug treatment] but
if the woman doesn't want that, it's no good.

(Assistant manager, Victoria House)

Working with residents who were not motivated to change was a source of
frustration for staff.

You take them because you want to help them but they aren't really
helping themselves.

(Assistant manager, Victoria House)

What is problematic is people who aren't motivated to change.

(Deputy manager, Carlton House)

At the same time, it was appreciated that residents should not be forced
into making changes to their lives and emphasised that residents needed to
make choices, supported by hostel staff about their future.

We do lots of different things but it's not always appropriate or they
don't always want to take it up.

(Assistant manager, Victoria House)

This approach was perceived as unproblematic for bailees but those on
probation were expected to deal with their offending behaviour and had
agreed to this by accepting the probation order.

We offer people opportunities to address some of the problems
highlighted on their assessment if they wish to and I stress if they
wish to. For the probationers, well they have chosen to deal with
their problems.

(Deputy manager, North Street Hostel)

Even if residents feel motivated to change and are able to appreciate the
ways in which hostel workers are able to offer support, success is
contingent on a resident's ability to ask for help.

Sure I've seen success stories and it's brilliant when that happens but
these are the women who are able to say I need help, please help me.
A lot of the time we're dealing with damaged women who are not
able to say that but we've just got to keep trying and trying.

(Assistant manager, Victoria House)

149

2   Timing

Hostel work is unpredictable. Success is in part contingent on the coalescing of the individual factors described above at the same time as their period of residence in a hostel. Timing is one key to success and perhaps as Shaw (1996) argues in relation to social work practice 'just sheer luck'. If the timing is not right, success is unlikely as an assistant manager at Victoria House described.

> You might have a woman who has disclosed abuse. You pick up the phone and organise counselling. It's happened to me but the women have sometimes messed up and didn't go. It's so frustrating and it's all because the woman wasn't ready.

This does not mean hostel workers are powerless to act. Instead, they need to continue to work with people, help them to deal with immediate problems and explore with them possible ways forward.

> It's not the way we work with them that is wrong. It's just that part of what we do is a containment exercise waiting for the time when they are really ready to move on to something. Sometimes people are ready to move on. Other times you have to keep plugging away at it.
>
> (Assistant manager, Harding House)

3   Time

The process of 'plugging away' described by the Assistant manager at Harding House above takes time. This is frequently in short supply in hostels. Not only are staff resources limited but residents may only be in the hostel for a short period of time, especially those on bail. Lengths of residence will vary significantly because residents may leave before the trial (bailed elsewhere, remanded in custody, moved to another hostel), and those charged with serious offences will have to wait significantly longer for their case to proceed to the trial stage.

> They are only with us for a short period of time, three weeks, a month and it is very difficult.
>
> (Night support worker, Harding House)

150

A commonly held view was that the success was more likely with residents on probation. In part this can be attributed to time but the fact that probationers have chosen to reside in a hostel, albeit a severely constrained choice (i.e. hostel or prison), is influential.

> We've has some wonderful successes with women on a probation order, women charged with quite serious offences who've been with us a long time and if we manage to keep them out of custody through being acquitted or getting them a community order of some kind, that's a success.
>
> (Deputy manager, Victoria House)

> For people who are here for a long time, the quality of our work shows through.
>
> (Deputy manager, North Street Hostel)

> If someone is on probation, well you've got loads of time to talk about issues.
>
> (Assistant manager, North Street Hostel)

In their accounts, staff frequently spoke about an optimum amount of time that residents should spend in hostels. Unlimited time is not necessarily the key to success because hostels are limited in terms of the support that can provide:

> Hostels have an effect on people and for some people it takes three months and for others a much shorter time is enough and after that you are not doing them any good really because we don't do specialist stuff.
>
> (Assistant manager, North Street Hostel)

> If someone leaves badly I tend to think that they have had their time at the hostel and we have done as much for them as we can.
>
> (Assistant manager, North Street Hostel)

4   Limits to hostel work

Hostel staff continually referred to their limitations of their knowledge and expertise. To use a medical analogy, they saw themselves in a similar role to general practitioners: a first port of call but with the ability to identify potential problems and refer people to specialists as and when necessary.

> If you work with somebody and have brought all their stuff to the surface, they need to go somewhere else to get some more specific and intensive work. We can't offer that because we are catering for a whole range of people.
>
> (Assistant manager, North Street Hostel)

> We're not specialist in anything. We are the first point of contact. We can give advice on where to go but we can't actually do anything ourselves.
>
> (Assistant manager, Victoria House)

> You are not the experts. You can only help so much but there are professionals there who can.
>
> (Assistant manager, Carlton House)

In particular, staff tended to feel out of their depth when faced with problems relating to substance use and physical, sexual and emotional abuse. The latter was of particular concern in the three hostels which accommodated women. Whilst they were willing to help residents as far as possible, they were keen to emphasise the limitations and draw firm boundaries about how far they could support residents.

> We are not trained as counsellors but we are limited in what we can do.
>
> (Assistant manager, Victoria House)

> I don't mind sitting listening to them but if they expect me to give anything back, I'm really not able to. But I can give them information about where to go and help them to follow that up.
>
> (Assistant manager, North Street Hostel)

5   External factors

> But a lot of it is social policy and economic policy which affects people's lives.
>
> (Assistant Manager, Harding House)

Hostels can play an important part in offering support to offenders and helping them to make changes to their lives but ultimately the ability of hostels to offer support is subverted through the lack of ongoing support and social and economic policies which fail to support some of the most socially excluded people in society. Drakeford and Vanstone (1996a) argue that without concerted efforts to address the social circumstances of those people who appear before the courts, attempts to influence their individual offending will meet with only limited success. Focusing on poverty, employment and training, housing and health they recognise the limitations of the political focus on individual responsibility and emphasise the need to tackle the social contexts within which offending is produced.

Coping with feelings of failure

Whilst staff were able to provide examples of their work which had gone particularly well, these were often viewed by staff as exceptions rather than the norm. When staff have high expectations of what can be achieved, individual workers may experience feelings of failure when the gap between expectations and reality is wide. A number of workers, particular those new to hostel work, expressed these feelings when asked about the extent to which they felt successful in their work. An assistant manager at Victoria House discussed at length how she often experienced feelings of failure.

> I think that's one of the areas where I'm useless. My definition of success would be getting the women through the bail period successfully; not re-offending, getting back before curfew, she hasn't got any issues that haven't been dealt with and that's rare. For me, that is a problem. I go home thinking oh no, so and so has been arrested because they got into a fight . . . When I have supervision, one of the things that comes out is the success bit. I don't see the success at all.
>
> (Assistant manager, Victoria House)

The assistant manager at Victoria House, quoted above, went on to illustrate her point by referring to work with one client which she felt had gone particularly badly.

153

We had one really chaotic woman and I was her keyworker and I felt that I was really failing this woman. I went to my manager and said what can I do? She said you have done this and you done that. It literally is basic things like I'm saying a roof over their heads and you measure success in a very basic way.

(Assistant manager, Victoria House)

In the above instance, supervision with the manager performed a number of functions. It emphasised to the assistant manager the need for realism and to recognise the difficulties and challenges faced by workers when working with individuals with multiple and complex problems. In this way it helped her to cope with feelings of perceived failure and to derive job satisfaction by appreciating that some of her actions, however small, had made a difference to the lives of offenders they worked with. The supervision provided an explanation for a problem – the difficulties of working with the client group and a professional safety net – ways of coping with perceived failure (c.f. Shaw and Shaw, 1999).

Earlier in this chapter we explored hostel workers' suggestions that effective work was facilitated by the coalescing of a number of factors such as sufficient time and appropriate timing. Limited success can therefore be accounted for by the absence of these factors and appreciating the limits of hostel work and the influence of external policy. Through this means, failure was excused rather than personalised

Concluding comments

Exploration of the meaning of success among hostel workers revealed clear discrepancies between official criteria and their own definitions. This may relate to a deeper tension abut the purposes and priorities of hostels as discussed in chapter three, but crucially it reflects staff's perceptions that official criteria do not recognise the day-to-day realities of practice.

Analysis of the hostel workers accounts' then reveals many common themes with Shaw (1996) research on social workers. Like social workers, hostels workers appear to have two contrasting 'models' of evaluation – 'evaluation proper' and self-evaluation of their work with residents for whom they were responsible. The former is perceived as formal, time consuming and as scrutiny from above. Success is measured quantitatively and this form of performance measure is driven by management concerns.

In contrast, self-evaluating emphasises quality and worth and appreciates evaluation has to draw upon complex evidence which is difficult to interpret. It recognises that progress is typically achieved through slow, incremental steps and therefore a long-term view is necessary. This can be described as 'on your feet' evaluation. Time is rarely put aside for this form of evaluation, although it is done implicitly in informal conversations, team meetings and supervisions.

Using the hostel workers' accounts, we can locate the effectiveness of hostel work in the realities of day-to-day practice. The danger attached to some models of evaluation is that they impose an abstract and decontextualised framework of evaluation and therefore lack meaning in the context of everyday work within bail and probation hostels. Developing alternative ways of evaluating practice helps to create hostel work as meaningful and purposeful, even in the face of perceived failure when judged by official criteria. Evaluation can then be viewed as a means of development and knowledge generation rather than accountability (see Chelimsky, 1997). By combining official and staff criteria for success we can answer more fully key questions about hostel provision: do hostels enable individuals to make changes to their lives? Is hostel provision accommodation being used to its full potential?

9 Concluding Comments

In the preceding chapters an ethnographic account has been provided of working in hostels for offenders. 'Thick description' (Geertz, 1973), organised around analytic frameworks, has been utilised to build up a collective picture of the everyday, the banal and the commonplace within hostel for offenders, as well as the unique and the extraordinary. In this way the account tried to capture the voices of hostel workers by documenting their own experiences in their own words. The final chapter draws out recurring themes within this ethnographic account. It also explores implications of the research for framing future policy, and for methodological debates.

Recurring themes

Throughout this text, the case study of residential work with offenders in approved hostels has been used to reflect upon wider changes in criminal justice and social policy. These include the march of managerialism, an enhanced commitment to assessing and managing risk and an interest in effective practice. We have explored some of the difficulties of translating these ideas into work in residential settings, and it has been frequently suggested that the realities of hostel work are not fully appreciated by colleagues in the Probation Service and criminal justice policy makers.

Throughout this text it has also been suggested that the combination of working with a difficult client group in a difficult setting creates a unique blend of professional and personal anxieties for workers. Residential work with offenders is thus demanding yet paradoxically is not always recognised as such by the Probation Service as a whole. Certainly this is a widely held view by those interviewed as part of this project and those included in the latest thematic inspection (HM Inspectorate of Probation, 1998). The low status of residential work may not always be explicitly stated by probation officers rather translated into their day-to-day practices such as attempts by some probation officers to refer unsuitable clients to hostels. Faced with feelings of isolation from the Probation Service, hostel workers therefore secure a sense of identity and validation from their immediate colleagues in the hostel team. Hostel work is in essence team work, and team building should be encouraged. However, as hostels move towards playing a key role in the supervision of 'risky' offenders at all stages in their criminal justice process, negative attitudes to residential work are not only inappropriate but are also a threat to effective practice with such offenders. Developing links between field and residential workers should be a priority for individual probation services. This might help to widen access to training, professional development and support groups for residential workers.

The value of support systems has also been stressed in the preceding chapters. The workers interviewed demonstrated commitment and enthusiasm about their work but always acknowledged some of the more negative aspects of hostel work. Residential work with offenders can be described as stressful, emotionally draining, sometimes dangerous and always potentially risky. Unsurprisingly such work can be daunting for novices, particularly as the successes of their efforts are not always readily apparent. Support, in varying forms, therefore is essential to all those workers in hostels throughout their careers. This requires action by individual hostels, the National Probation Service and the Home Office.

Hostel workers' reflections on the inappropriateness of their working environment have also been highlighted throughout the book. None of the hostels were purpose built and each had its particular drawbacks. At first glance the design and layout of the hostel may seem a trivial point but it has far-reaching implications. Poorly designed hostels can be potentially risky ones, they may offer little comfort for staff who wish to take a break, and they may provide no suitable private accommodation for staff supervision or for keyworking residents. The design of future hostels could usefully draw upon the perspective of those currently working in other hostels.

The theme of social inclusion has also permeated the individual chapters. Current criminal justice thinking may be preoccupied with a commitment to engaging offenders in programmes based on 'what works' principles, but hostel workers interviewed emphasised tackling the multiple and complex problems experienced by residents which may or may not be related to their offending. In other words, their work is focused on the needs of offender. For those on bail at least, work to address their needs is largely client-led. Related to the concern with promoting social inclusion is the recognition of the different needs of different client groups. This has been explored throughout, mainly with reference to work with female offenders, and by exploring the advantages and disadvantages of single-sex and mixed provision. The role of hostels in promoting the social inclusion and ensuring equality of opportunity merits further attention, particularly at a national level.

The key themes which emerged from the research have been delineated, and the reader has been offered a flavour of what it is like to work with offenders in a residential setting. This chapter now turns to a discussion of the implications of the research, beginning first with suggestions as to how the findings could inform future policy.

Implications for policy and practice

It is important to remind the reader that this text recounts the findings of a small-scale study based on a small number of hostels. It was essentially exploratory. The findings are based on qualitative data which is often characterised as being strong in terms of validity rather than generalisability. The strengths of the data include completeness, plausibility, illustrativeness, understanding and responsiveness to experience. The depth of the findings are emphasised over their wider applicability. Nonetheless the study did include a range of different hostels and thus it is hoped that the research will have wider implications for policy and practice. At the end of each chapter we have explored specific policy recommendations, and further suggestions have been included in this chapter. These have included recommendations for individual approved hostels, the National Probation Service and the Home Office. Rather than repeat these here, this section will critically reflect, albeit briefly, on the relationship between research, policy and practice.

Based on research findings policy recommendations can be made, but as Hammersley (1992, p.133) argues:

> Research cannot produce knowledge that can simply be applied to resolve practical problems . . . Research cannot substitute for experience here, though it can inform it. Indeed, research findings must be assessed by practitioners in the light of their own experiences and used in relation to their contextual knowledge and practical judgement.

Hammersley's arguments problematise the relationship between research and policy. What also needs to be acknowledged is that social research, particularly criminological research, is a deeply politicised process. Consequently, many research findings do not resonate comfortable with dominant political ideologies of law and order (Hughes, 1996). Research may have an impact on policy in a more indirect way. For example, if practitioners in the four hostels studied began to think more critically about their practice, then an important contribution to developing residential work with offenders has been made. Indeed in some of the interviews hostel workers came up with suggestions for how residential work with offenders could be improved which they planned to take further. For example,

> If we had a chance to meet once a week for three-quarters of an hour to discuss actual scenarios and how we handled it, how we interpreted the rules on that so we had a consensus and some consistency . . . that would be brilliant. I'll mention that at the next staff meeting.

> (Assistant manager, North Street Hostel)

In addition, frequently the question 'what do other hostels do?' was posed, and thus the research project also acted as a way of disseminating good practice between hostels. As discussed in chapter four, hostel workers often experience feelings of isolation and detachment, and thus were eager to learn more about the strategies used by other hostel workers to manage residential work with offenders.

Methodological reflections

Qualitative researchers often make a double contribution when they conduct their research. They contribute towards methodological debates as well as contributing to our understanding of the subject matter they choose to study. Elsewhere I have explored some of the methodological issues arising from the research. These include the emotional nature of qualitative research (Wincup, 2001b), the compatibility between feminist perspectives and ethnographic approaches (Wincup, 1999b) and issues of access (Smith and Wincup, 2000). Here the focus is on the appropriateness of the research methods selected, and the importance of qualitative approaches to evaluation.

Qualitative research is not without controversies and dilemmas, and indeed numerous questions are raised through the research process which require reflection upon. Such reflections can be used in ways to enhance qualitative studies rather than downgrade them. Qualitative approaches to research contains enormous potential to make visible the experiences of criminal justice professionals. In the research studies reported in this volume, the blend of different research methodologies worked well. Through participant observation, I was able to build up rapport with research participants and to get a sense of the key issues relevant to residential workers' experiences of working with offenders, and the everyday world of approved hostels. Through interviews I was able to ask questions on emergent themes from the observational period of the research. Reflecting on the data I have leads me to argue that the complexities and problems associated with residential work with offenders are sufficiently great that multiple methods via qualitative research are required. The staff I interviewed endorsed my choice of methods.

> You could ask me what I've been doing in the last half hour and I'd say looking at a map and doing some sums, but it means nothing unless you know that a resident has been offered a job and needs to know how to get there and if they would be better off than if they were claiming benefits.
>
> (Fieldnotes, North Street Hostel)

Posing different evaluation questions would have enabled me to discover alternative aspects of residential work with offenders. This study should therefore be viewed as part of a patchwork of knowledge. It could be complemented by qualitative studies of how hostels are experienced by residents (see Wincup, 1997), by ex-residents, by the criminal courts and by other criminal justice professionals.

Future research

Following in the footsteps of many academic texts, this one ends with a call for further research. The majority of contemporary criminologists interested in punishment have focused on the mysterious, perhaps exotic, world of imprisonment. This world, isolated from wider society, offers a source of endless fascination for criminologists (see King, 2000). In contrast research on community penalties is not so appealing (Mair, 2000). Residential work with offenders has been particularly neglected, especially during the past two decades. At the time of writing the Home Office has invited bids for an evaluation of 'pathfinder' or pilot programmes which have been designed to test different regimes for approved bail and probation hostels. Whilst this injection of funding for research on approved hostels is welcomed the topic is narrowly defined. We also need to understand basic practices in order to provide a better grounding for policy. This includes capturing the experiences of those who reside in approved hostels, as well as those of residential workers.

My own motivation for studying approved hostels stemmed in part from a concern that researchers need to go beyond highlighting flaws within British prisons and making suggestions for reform. At the same time as helping to make prisons better places, researchers need to consider alternatives to custodial sentences and remands in custody. A useful starting place would be to explore current alternatives to custody, namely approved bail and probation hostels.

Appendix A

Extract taken from Home Office (1995) *National Standards for the Supervision of Offenders in the Community*, Home Office, London. Section 8, pages 56-61.

The management of approved probation and bail hostels

Introduction

This National standard deals with the management of approved probation and bail hostels. It should be read in conjunction with other National Standards and also with the Approved Probation and Bail Hostel Rules 1995. This standard applies equally to approved hostels run by probation committees and those which have a voluntary management committee so that whenever term 'committee' is used, this should be taken as referring to the area probation committee or the management committee, as appropriate, unless specified otherwise.

2. This standard provides a set of fundamental requirements for the management of approved hostels in England and Wales. Its purpose is to provide a basis for the confidence of the courts and the public in approved hostels; to provide a structure for the development of good practice in each probation area; and to promote efficient and effective standards of service delivery.

3. The area probation committee should satisfy itself that this standard is complied with in the hostels that it provides. The voluntary management committee should do the same for the voluntary managed hostels for which it is responsible.

4. Committees should also satisfy themselves that hostels, including cluster properties, met the appropriate standards of housing, health

and safety, food and hygiene and other relevant legislation. Their responsibilities extend to both the staff and residents of the hostel.

Purpose of approved hostels

5. The purpose of approved hostels is to provide an advanced level of supervision to enable certain bailees and offenders to remain under supervision in the community. Hostel residents should be expected to go to work or to attend projects, training courses or treatment facilities in the community. It follows that approved hostels should have close links with, and form part of, the probation committees' strategy for the supervision of bailees and offenders in the community, including partnership arrangements.

6. Approved hostels should be reserved for those who require this advanced supervision and are not meant simply as accommodation. They should provide a supportive and structured environment within which their residents can be supervised effectively. But it should be clearly understood that approved hostels are not secure and so, unlike Prison Service establishments, cannot provide the same degree of protection from the risks posed by the most serious offenders.

7. Hostel staff should develop a regime in agreement with their committee and the probation service locally. This should be set out in a published statement of aims and objectives which should seek to:

- ensure that the requirements of the courts are met
- promote a responsible and law-abiding lifestyle and respect for others
- create and maintain a constructive relationship between the hostel's staff and residents
- facilitate the work of the probation service and other agencies aimed at reducing the risk that hostel residents will often or re-offend in future
- assist hostel residents to keep or find employment and to develop their employment skills

163

- encourage and enable hostel residents to use the facilities available in the local community and to develop their ability to become self-reliant in doing so
- enable hostel residents to move on successfully to other appropriate accommodation at the end of their period of residence
- establish and maintain good relations with neighbours and the community in general.

Information to courts and other agencies

8. The Chief Probation Officer (CPO) should encourage judges, magistrates and representatives of other criminal justice agencies in their areas to visit approved hostels so that they may see for themselves how the hostels operate, what they have to offer and the kind of residents to whom they are best suited.

9. Additionally, the committee should provide the courts in its local and neighbouring areas and its referring agencies, especially Bail Information Officers, with information about the hostel setting out:

- its statement of aims and objectives
- the rules of the hostel to which the residents will be required to adhere
- the number of spaces available
- its policy and practice for the use of clusters
- the method of referral
- its criteria for accepting clients
- its hours within which the residents are required to reside within the hostel
- its breach policy
- its equal opportunities policy
- its move-on policy when the resident no longer requires the supervision provided by an approved hostel.

Information to prospective residents

10. The committee should also provide written information for prospective residents explaining what they can expect from the hostel and what will be expected of them. Consideration should also

be given to providing this information in appropriate minority languages.

Admissions policy

11.　There should be for each hostel a policy, approved by the relevant probation service, setting out the categories of resident who may safely and appropriately be accommodated there. But the decision to make a condition of residence as part of a bail or probation order is entirely the responsibility of the court and must be given effect on the basis that such a condition can be rescinded only be a further order of the court.

12.　Subject to the availability of places, hostel staff should give priority to those who both require and will benefit from the structured and supportive environment provided. The hostel should seek not to accept prospective residents:

- who are charged with or convicted of offences too minor to justify a placement in an approved hostel
- whose admission would present an unacceptable risk of serious harm to the staff, other residents, or the immediate community
- whose admission might place that person at risk from other residents
- whose sole need is accommodation, and who do not require the level of supervision provided at an approved hostel. An exception may however be made in the case of someone who is homeless and would otherwise be remanded in custody, on the understanding that arrangements will be made to assess that person quickly and obtain appropriate alternative accommodation without delay.

Induction of residents

13.　The rules should be clearly explained to each new resident on arrival together with the action which will be taken if the resident fails to comply (see paragraph 21). Prospective residents should have been informed of the rules of the hostel before arrival and agree to abide by them. A member of the hostel staff should verify that this has been done and, if necessary, clarify any misunderstanding.

14.   Hostel staff should arrange for all residents, as soon as possible after their arrival, to be offered support to address their personal needs (e.g. medical problems, access to benefit).

15.   Hostel staff should ensure that they receive a copy of the relevant court order or licence and that the details are correct. They should also obtain the personal information required in paragraph 27 and ensure that it is properly recorded.

16.   When the supervising officer is not a member of the hostel staff, hostel staff should notify the probation service of the admission of each resident required to reside there as part of a probation order or subject to post-release supervision.

Rules of the hostel

17.   The committee should draw up a set of rules for the hostel detailing the requirements and restrictions on residents when they are on the premises, including the hostel grounds and any cluster properties. These should be permanently displayed in the hostel and consideration should be given as to whether they should be made available in appropriate minority languages. The rules should prohibit:

- violent, threatening or disruptive language or conduct
- disorderly, threatening or abusive behaviour as a result of drink or drug abuse
- the use of controlled drugs, other than on prescription and following notification to hostel staff
- any conduct or language which might reasonably give serious offence to hostel staff, residents or members of the public
- theft or damage to the property of the hostel, staff or other residents.

18.   The rule of the hostel should require the payment of the agreed weekly charge by the resident when due, except in the circumstances when this payment may be waived.

Supervision and enforcement

Residence requirement

19.   There should be a requirement for all residents to return to the hostel by a fixed time each evening and to remain in the hostel until 6.00am. The latest fixed time by which residents must return is 11.00pm: this may be earlier in the light of local circumstances, or exceptionally extended to 11.30pm. All residents on bail should be required to abide by this rule unless the court orders otherwise. In the cases of other residents, the hostel manger may give a dispensation in certain circumstances, for example, if the resident is doing shift work, after consulting the supervising officer where appropriate.

20.   For residents on probation, any failure to return to the hostel by the required time without an acceptable excuse should be the subject of a formal warning, as set out in the probation order National Standard. In line with that standard, no more than two formal warnings can be given before breach action is instituted. Similar criteria should be applied to those on bail.

21.   Serious or repeated infringement of the rules of the hostel constitutes a breach of the residence requirement. If the resident is subject to a probation order, this should be reported to the supervising officer and dealt with in accordance with the relevant National Standard.

Residents on probation

22.   In respect of residents on probation, hostel staff should work with the supervising officer and the resident to put together a programme for the duration of the period of residence, which meets the requirements of the National Standard for probation order supervision. The programme should:

•   complement the probation order supervision and the requirements of other community orders to which the resident may be subject as far as possible

- not conflict with the requirements of full-time or part-time employment, education or training in which the resident is currently engaged, and where appropriate, the observance of religious beliefs
- be subject to review during the periods of residence in the light of the resident's progress
- provide and plan for the resident's eventual discharge from the hostel.

Residents on bail

23. In respect of residents on bail, the hostel staff should:

- ensure that residents comply with any requirements imposed by the courts while they are on hostel premises, including clusters and the grounds
- ensure that, where available, residents are offered a place on any programme on how to avoid offending
- provide a contribution to any report to the court, including a pre-sentence report, based on an assessment of the resident while at the hostel.

24. Hostel staff should notify the police and the court of any serious or repeated instances of failure of a resident to comply with the requirements of his or her bail including compliance with the rules of the hostel. Hostel staff should also notify the police if a resident on bail fails to arrive or is known to have committed a further offence. In all such instances, the police should be notified the same day.

25. Any written assessment of residents on bail that hostel staff make should include details of any serious or repeated failure to comply with the requirements of the court order and the rules of the hostel.

Residents under post-release supervision

26. The National Standard on supervision before or after release from custody sets out the procedures to be followed in the enforcement of licences. Hostel staff should work with the supervising officer to ensure the provision of programme of supervision and support for

resident's needs, which meet the requirements of the National Standard for supervision before and after release from custody.

Information to be recorded

27.   Hostel staff must record the following information about each resident on arrival:

* name, home address, last known address, charge or conviction resulting in the residence requirement, sentence/licence plus additional requirements, and, where appropriate, supervising probation officer
* date of birth, gender and ethnic group
* previous criminal record (if any)
* name and address of next of kin and of any dependants
* prescribed medication, medical conditions, diet
* the sentencing court, supervising court and paying authority
* date of return to court (if any).

The hostel should also keep a copy of the court order or licence under which the resident is required to reside at the hostel.

28.   Hostel staff should maintain a formal record of significant daily events, including violent incidents and failure to comply with the rules of the hostel. A separate record may be kept of more informal staff observations and notes. Confidentiality of records and other information about residents should be maintained having regard to the need to protect the public and the need to serve the courts, and work with the police and other agencies for the proper functioning of the criminal justice system as a whole.

29.   A voluntary management committee should send the CPO for the area in which the hostel is situated a copy of all statistical returns required by the Secretary of State.

Performance monitoring

30. The committee should make arrangements for the regular monitoring of the hostel's operational performance. This should include making arrangements for visits and inspections.

31. The CPO should present to the probation committee at least annually information about the outcome of referrals to approved hostels in the probation area. This should include the number of referrals made; the number of bailees; the number of probation orders with a requirement of residence; the number of bailees; the number of probation orders with a requirement of residence; the number on post-release supervision; the number of residents whose period of residence was successfully completed; and the number whose period of residence was terminated early and why. The report should also cover the implementation of health and safety and equal opportunities policies and a summary of serious incidents.

Appendix B

Extract taken from Home Office (2000) *National Standards for the Supervision of Offenders in the Community*, Home Office, London.

Section E: Approved Hostels

Purpose

E1.   The purpose of approved hostels is to provide an enhanced level of residential supervision with the aim of protecting the public by reducing the likelihood of offending. Approved hostels are for bailees, probationers and post-custody licencees, where their risk of causing serious harm to the public or other likelihood of reoffending means that no other form of accommodation in the community would be suitable.

E2.   Approved hostels enhance supervision in that they:

*   impose a supervised nighttime curfew which can be extended to other times of the day (e.g. as required by a court order or licence condition);

*   provide 24 hour staff oversight;

*   undertake ongoing assessment of attitudes and behaviour;

*   require compliance with clearly stated house rules which are rigorously enforced;

*   provide a programme of regular supervision, support and daily monitoring that tackles offending behaviour and reduces risks.

Rules

E3.   In addition to these Standards, hostels shall operate within:

•   the Approved Probation and Bail Hostel Rules 1995;

•   a set of local house rules detailing the requirements and restrictions on residents. These shall include requirements and prohibitions on:

•   the use of alcohol, solvents and controlled drugs, other than on prescription and following notification to hostel staff;

•   any conduct or language that reasonably give serious offence to hostel staff, other residents or members of the public;

•   theft of, or damage to, the property of the hostel, staff, electronic monitoring contractors or residents; and shall also:

•   require residents to be in the hostel between 23.00 and 06.00;

•   require prompt payment of the weekly charge.

Admission policy

E4.   Hostel staff must respond to each referral as soon as possible. Hostel admissions shall be based on risk assessment procedures, using the relevant elements of OASys, when implemented, which:

•   do not automatically exclude any particular category of offence;

•   identify the risk of serious harm to the public, hostel staff, the individual or other hostel residents;

•   reflect the ability of the hostel to manage and reduce the risks identified in accordance with local public protection policies and practices; and

•   reduce the likelihood of reoffending.

Supervision

E5.   Supervision in the hostel shall:

•   address and reduce offending behaviour;

•   challenge offenders to accept responsibility for the crimes committed and their consequences;

•   contribute to the protection of the public;

•   motivate and assist residents towards a greater sense of personal responsibility and discipline; and

•   aid reintegration of offenders as law-abiding members of the community.

E6.   All hostel residents must have a written assessment in relation to the risks they present of causing serious harm to victim(s) of the offence, to the public, to the staff or to themselves.

E7.   Hostel staff shall:

•   ensure that, as soon as practicable after arrival, every new resident is interviewed by a member of the supervisory staff when the house rules will be explained fully, and signed by the resident;

•   within seven working days of each resident's arrival, and based on the assessment of the resident, produce a planned programme for the expected duration of the stay at the hostel which:

•   addresses offending behaviour;

•   is congruent with any other orders to which the resident may be subject;

•   addresses the management of identified risks of harm posed by the resident;

173

- does not conflict with any reasonable employment requirements or the offender's religious considerations;

- ensure that residents take part in hostel-run or other programmes on how to avoid offending. Programmes should be designed according to the principles of effective practice;

- plan for the resident's community reintegration, including arrangements for the resident's discharge from the hostel; and

- contribute to any report to the court on the resident and include details of any serious or repeated failure to comply with the court order or the rules of the hostel, as well as achievements.

E8.   For offenders subject to statutory supervision there must be a supervision plan, as identified in section C of these Standards. Sometimes this will be the responsibility of hostel staff, sometimes of the supervising probation officer located elsewhere, in which case a copy must be made available to the hostel manager once the plan, and any reviews, are completed. Any hostel programme for a resident must be consistent with a supervision plan.

Recording

E9.   In addition to the general recording requirements of these National Standards, hostel staff shall record the following information in respect of each resident on arrival:

- name, date of birth, sex, ethnicity, home address, next of kin (with address and telephone number);

- sentencing court, and charge or conviction resulting in residence requirement;

- any bail, order or licence conditions;

- any future court dates and reports required;

- any supervising probation officer;

174

- any religious or cultural considerations;

- any prescribed medication, medical conditions, diet, etc; and

- the paying authority.

E10. Staff must subsequently record any changes to these items plus any significant events, including violent or racist incidents and failure to comply with the rules, in the resident's records. In addition, hostels are required to keep up to date a logbook in which significant incidents, and complaints, are to be recorded.

Enforcement

E11. Hostel staff shall:

- ensure that residents comply with all requirements imposed by the courts or included in their licence;

- notify the police of any serious or repeated instances of failure of a resident to comply with any requirements, including compliance with the house rules; and

- notify the police immediately if any resident on bail either fails to arrive or any resident commits a further offence.

E12. Each hostel shall have a clear policy in respect of enforcement of the house rules. Minor infringements of the house rules may be dealt with by informal local warnings, which must be recorded. However, serious or repeated breaches will result in recall to prison, breach action, or application for revocation of bail as appropriate. Staff are to be guided in their judgements by the requirements in these Standards concerning enforcement (see Section D).

Arrangements for electronic monitoring

E13. Hostel management, in conjunction with contractors, shall ensure that:

- they follow a protocol agreed with the contractors for dealing with curfew variations and violations where electronic monitoring has been imposed as a condition of a parole licence or with a curfew order;

- residents subject to electronic monitoring are fully conversant with the operation of the equipment and understand the curfew conditions imposed; and

- arrangements are in place to enable 24 hour access to the hostel by contractors.

References

Ablitt, F. (2000), 'Community Penalties for Women – The Need for Evidence', *Criminal Justice Matters*, no. 39, pp.12-13.

Allen, H. (1987), *Justice Unbalanced: Gender, Psychiatry and Judicial Decisions*, Open University Press, Buckingham.

Anon (1993), 'My Life as a Woman in a Bail Hostel', *Probation Journal*, vol. 40, pp.149-50.

Antaki, C. (ed) (1988), *Analysing Everyday Explanations: A Casebook of Methods*, Sage, London.

Ash, E. (1995), 'Taking Account of Feelings', in Pritchard, J. (ed), *Good Practice in Supervision*, Jessica Kingsley Publishers, London.

Ashworth, A. (1998), *The Criminal Process: An Evaluative Study*, Oxford University Press, Oxford.

Atherton, J. (1986), *Professional Supervision in Group Care*, Tavistock, London.

Atkinson, P. (1981), *The Clinical Experience: The Construction and Reconstruction of Medical Reality*, Gower, Aldershot.

Atkinson, P. (1983) 'The Reproduction of Professional Communities', in Dingwall, R. and Lewis, P. (eds), *The Sociology of the Professions*, Macmillan, London.

Atkinson, P. and Delamont, S. (1985), 'Socialisation into Teaching: The Research which Lost its Way', *British Journal of Sociology of Education*, vol. 6, pp.307-22.

Atkinson, P. and Delamont, S. (1990), 'Professions and Powerlessness: Female Marginality in the Learned Occupations', *Sociological Review*, vol. 38, pp.307-22.

Balloch, S., Pahl, J. and McLean, J. (1998), 'Working in the Social Services: Job Satisfaction, Stress and Violence', *British Journal of Social Work*, vol. 28, pp.329-50.

Barry, K. (1991), *Probation Hostels and their Regimes*, Institute of Criminology, Cambridge.

Beaumont, B. and Mistry, T. (1996), 'Doing a Good Job Under Duress', *Probation Journal*, vol. 43, pp.200-24.

Becker, H., Geer, B., Hughes, E. and Strauss, A. (1961), *Boys in White: Student Culture in Medical School*, University of Chicago Press, Chicago.

Bennett, P., Evans, R. and Tattersall, A. (1993), 'Stress and Coping in Social Workers: A Preliminary Investigation', *British Journal of Social Work*, vol. 23, pp.31-44.

Berk, S. (1980), *Women and Household Labour*, Sage, London.

Boswell, G. (1989), *Holding the Balance Between Court and Client*, University of East Anglia, Norwich.

Brannen, J. and Moss, P. (1991), *Managing Mothers*, Macmillan, Basingstoke.

Britton, J. and Pamneja, T. (2000), *Homelessness and Drugs: Managing Incidents*, Drugscope, London.

Brookman, F., Noaks, L. and Wincup, E. (2001), 'Access to Justice: Remand Issues and the Human Rights Act', *Probation Journal*, vol. 48, pp.195-202.

Brown, A. and Bourne, I. (1996), *The Social Work Supervisor*, Open University Press, Buckingham.

Brown, G. and Geelan, S. (1998), 'Elliot House: Working with Mentally Disordered Offenders', *Probation Journal*, vol. 45, pp.10-14.

Brown, J. and Campbell, E. (1994), *Stress and Policing*, John Wiley, Chichester.

Brownlee, I. (1998), *Community Punishment: A Critical Introduction*, Longman, London.

Buchanan, J. and Miller, M. (1995), 'Probation: A Crisis of Identity', *Probation Journal*, vol. 42, pp.195-98.

Buchanan, J. and Miller, M. (1997), 'Reclaiming a Social Work Identity' for Probation', *Probation Journal*, vol. 44, pp.32-36.

Bucher, R. and Stelling, J. (1977), *Becoming Professional*, Sage, Beverley Hills, Ca.

Buckley, K. and Wilson, C. (1989), 'Empowering Women', *Probation Journal*, vol. 36, pp.165-70.

Budd, T. (1999), *Violence at Work: Findings from the British Crime Survey*, Home Office, London.

Bull, R. and Shaw, I. (1992), 'Constructing Causal Accounts in Social Work', *Sociology*, vol. 26, pp.533-49.

Butler, I. and Drakeford, M. (2001), 'Tough Enough? Youth Justice Under New Labour', Probation Journal, vol. 48, pp.119-24.

Carlen, P. (1985), *Criminal Women: Autobiographical Accounts*, Polity Press, Cambridge.

Carlen, P. (1988), *Women, Crime and Poverty*, Open University Press, Milton Keynes.

Carlen, P. (1990), *Alternatives to Women's Imprisonment*, Open University Press, Buckingham.

Carlen, P. (1996), *Jigsaw: A Political Criminology of Youth Homelessness*, Open University Press, Buckingham.

Carlen, P. (1998), *Sledgehammer: Women's Imprisonment at the Millennium*, Macmillan, Basingstoke.

Cavanagh, K. and Cree, V. (eds) (1996) *Working with Men: Feminism and Social Work*, Routledge, London.

Cavendish, R. (1982), *Women on the Line*, Routledge and Kegan Paul, London.

Cavadino, M. and Dignan, J. (1997), *The Penal System: An Introduction*, Sage, London.

Cavadino, M., Crow, I. and Dignan, J. (1999), *Criminal Justice 2000*, Waterside Press, Winchester.

Central Council for Education and Training in Social Work (1973), *Training for Residential Work: Discussion Document*, CCETSW, London.

Chapman, T. and Hough, M. (1998), *Evidence Based Practice: A Guide to Effective Practice*, Home Office, London.

Cheetham, J., Fuller, R., McIvor, G. and Petch, A. (1992), *Evaluating Social Work Effectiveness*, Open University Press, Buckingham.

Chelimsky, E. (1997), 'Thoughts for a New Evaluation Society', *Evaluation*, vol. 3, pp.97-118.

Cherniss, C. (1980), *Staff Burnout*, Sage, London.

Coffey, A. (1994), *Collective Responsibility and Individual Success: The Early Training Experiences of Graduate Accountants*, Unpublished PhD thesis, Cardiff University.

Coffey, A. and Atkinson, P. (1996), *Making Sense of Qualitative Data*, Sage, London.

Colledge, M., Collier, P. and Brand, S. (1999), *Programmes for Offenders: Guidance for Evaluators*, Home Office, London.

Commission for Racial Equality (1990), *Bail Hostels and Racial Equality*, Commission for Racial Equality, London.

Crow, I. (1996), 'Employment, Training and Offending', in M. Drakeford and M. Vanstone (eds), *Beyond Offending Behaviour*, Ashgate, Aldershot.

Denney, D. (1992), *Racism and Anti-Racism in Probation*, Routledge, London.

Department of Health (1996), *The Task Force to Review Services for Drug Misusers*, Department of Health, London.

Dodgson, K., Goodwin, P., Howard, P., Llewellyn-Thomas, S., Mortimer, E., Russell, N. and Weiner, M. (2001), *Electronic Monitoring of Released Prisoners: An Evaluation of the Home Detention Curfew Scheme*, Home Office, London.

Dominelli, L., Jeffers, L., Jones, G., Sibanda, S. and Williams, B. (1995), *Anti-Racist Probation Practice*, Arena, Aldershot.

Dominelli, L. and McLeod, E. (1989), *Feminist Social Work*, Macmillan, Basingstoke.

Donohoe, P. (2000), 'The Probation Service for Tomorrow', *Criminal Justice Matters*, no. 39, pp.33-34.

Douglas, M. (1984), 'Foreword', in T. Collins and Bruce, T., *Staff Support and Staff Training*, Tavistock, London.

Drakeford, M. (2000), *Privatisation and Social Policy*, Longman, London.

Drakeford, M. and Vanstone, M. (1996a), *Beyond Offending Behaviour*, Arena, Aldershot.

Drakeford, M. and Vanstone, M. (1996b), 'Rescuing the Social', *Probation Journal*, vol.43, pp. 16-19.

du Gay (1996), *Consumption and Identity at Work*, Sage, London.

Eaton, M. (1986), *Justice for Women: Family, Court and Social Control*, Open University Press, Milton Keynes.

Eaton, M. (1993), *Women After Prison*, Buckingham, Open University Press.

Ellis, T. (2000), 'Enforcement Policy and Practice: Evidence-based or Rhetoric-based?', *Criminal Justice Matters*, no. 39, pp.6-7.

Feeley, S. and Simon, J. (1992), 'The New Penology: Notes on the Emerging Strategy of Corrections and its Implications', *Criminology*, vol. 30, pp.452-74.

Fergusson, R. (1994), 'Managerialism In Education', in Clarke, J., Cochrane, A. and McLaughlin, E. (eds), *Managing Social Policy*, Sage, London.

Fetterman, M. (1989), *Ethnography: Step by Step*, Sage, Newbury Park, Ca.

Fielding, N. (1984), *Probation Practice: Client Support Under Social Control*, Gower, Aldershot.

Fielding, N. (1994), 'Cop Canteen Culture', in Newburn, T. and Stanko, E. (eds), *Just Boys Doing the Business*, Routledge, London.

Fisher, R. and Wilson, C. (1982), *Authority or Freedom? Probation Hostels for Adults*, Gower, Aldershot.

Flannery, R. (1996) 'Violence in the Workplace 1970-1995: A Review of the Literature', *Aggression and Violent Behaviour*, vol. 1, pp.57-68.

Folkard, M., Smith, D. and Smith, D. (1976), *IMPACT: Intensive Matched Probation and After Care Treatment 2: The Results of an Experiment*, Home Office, London.

Frude, N., Honess, T. and Maguire, M. (1994), *CRIME-PICS II*, Michael and Associates, Cardiff.

Furnham, A. (1988), *Lay Theories: Everyday Understanding of the Problems of Social Sciences*, Pergamon Press, Oxford.

Gamarnikow, E., Morgan, D., Purvis, J. and Taylorson, D. (eds) (1983), *The Public and the Private*, Gower, Aldershot.

Geertz, C. (1973), 'Thick Description', in Geertz, C. (eds), *The Interpretation of Cultures*, Basic Books, New York.

Gelsthorpe, L. (1992), Social Inquiry Reports: Race and Gender Considerations, *Home Office Research Bulletin*, vol. 32, pp.17-22.

Goodwin, R. (1995), 'Merseyside Adelaide House Reasoning and Rehabilitation Project with Women', in Ross, R. and Ross, R. (eds), *Thinking Straight*, Air Training and Publications, Ottowa.

Greene, J. (1994) 'Qualitative Program Evaluation: Practice and Promise', in Denzin, N. and Lincoln, Y. (eds) *Handbook of Qualitative Research*, Sage, Newbury Park, Ca.

Griffin, N., Geelan, S. and Briscoe, J. (1997), *Evaluation of Elliot House*, West Midlands Probation Service and Reaside Clinic, Birmingham.

Grimwood, G. (1995), 'Equal Opportunities: Welcoming Diversity', *Prison Service Journal*, issue 97, pp.20-23.

Hammersley, M. (1992), *What's Wrong with Ethnography?*, Routledge, London.

Hammersley, M. and Atkinson, P. (1995), *Ethnography*, Routledge, London.

Hanmer, J. and Statham, D. (1988), *Women and Social Work*, Macmillan, London.

Hannah-Moffatt, K. and Shaw, M. (2000), 'Thinking about Cognitive Skills? Think Again', *Criminal Justice Matters*, no. 39, pp.8-9.

Hardiker, P. (1977), 'Social Work Ideologies in the Probation Service', *British Journal of Social Work*, vol. 7, pp.131-54.

Harre, R. and Secord, P. (1972), *The Explanation of Social Behaviour*, Basil Blackwell, London.

Haxby, D. (1978), *Probation: A Changing Service*, Constable, London.

Hay, A. (1998), 'Women Need Women', *Probation Journal*, vol. 45, pp.36-38.

Hearden, K. (1998), *Violence at Work*, United Trade Press Ltd., London.

Hedderman, C. and Gelsthorpe, L. (1997), *Understanding the Sentencing of Women*, Home Office Research Study 170, Home Office, London.

Hedderman, C. and Hough, M. (2000), 'Tightening up Probation: A Step Too Far?', *Criminal Justice Matters*, no. 39, p.5.

Heidensohn, F. (1997), 'Gender and Crime', in Maguire, M., Morgan, R. and Reiner, R. (eds), *The Oxford Handbook of Criminology*, Oxford University Press, Oxford.

Hirst, G. (1996), 'Moving Forward: How did we do that?', *Probation Journal*, vol. 43, pp.58-63.

HM Inspectorate of Prisons (1997), *Women in Prison: A Thematic Review by HM Chief Inspector of Prisons*, Home Office, London.

HM Inspectorate of Probation (1991), *Report on Women Offenders and Probation Service Provision*, Home Office, London.

HM Inspectorate of Probation (1993), *Approved Probation and Bail Hostels: Report of a Thematic Inspection*, Home Office, London.

HM Inspectorate of Probation (1996), *Review of Probation Service Provision for Women Offenders*, Home Office, London.

HM Inspectorate of Probation (1998), *Delivering an Enhanced Level of Community Supervision: Report of a Thematic Inspection on the Work of Approved Probation and Bail Hostels*, Home Office, London.

HM Prison Service (1992), Regimes for Women, Home Office, London.

Hochshild, A. (1989), *The Second Shift: Working Patterns and the Revolution at Home*, Viking Press, New York.

Home Office (1984), *Probation Service in England and Wales: Statement of National Objectives and Priorities*, Home Office, London.

Home Office (1988), *Punishment, Custody and the Community*, Home Office, London.

Home Office (1990), *Crime, Justice and Protecting the Public*, Home Office, London.

Home Office (1992), *National Standards for the Supervision of Offenders in the Community*, Home Office, London.

Home Office (1995), *National Standards for the Supervision of Offenders in the Community*, Home Office, London.

Home Office (1996), *Protecting the Public: The Government's Strategy on Crime*, Home Office, London.

Home Office (1997), *The Three Year Plan for the Probation Service*, Home Office, London.

Home Office (1999), *Statistics on Women and the Criminal Justice System*, Home Office, London.

Home Office (2000), *National Standards for the Supervision of Offenders in the Community*, Home Office, London.

Home Office (2001a), *Hostels for Offenders – What they are and What they do*, www.homeoffice.gov.uk.

Home Office (2001b), *Probation Statistics, England and Wales 1999*, Home Office, London.

Home Office (2001c), *Prison Population Brief, England and Wales, June 2001*, Home Office, London.

Hood, R. (1992), *Race and Sentencing*, Clarendon Press, Oxford.

Howden-Windell, J. and Clark, D. (1999), *Criminological Needs of Female Offenders: A Literature Review*, HM Prison Service, London.

HSE (2001), *Tackling Work-related Stress*, HSE, London.

Hughes, G. (1996), 'The Politics of Criminological Research', in R. Sapsford (ed), *Researching Crime and Criminal Justice*, Open University course material (D315), Milton Keynes.

Hughes, G. (2001), 'The Competing Logics of Community Sanctions: Welfare, Rehabilitation and Restorative Justice', in McLaughlin, E. and Muncie, J. (eds), *Controlling Crime*, Sage, London.

Humphrey, C. and Pease, K. (1992), 'Effectiveness Measurement in Probation: A View from the Troops', *Howard Journal*, vol. 31, pp.31-52.

Inner London Probation Service (1994a), *The Residents' Report*, Inner London Probation Service, London.

Inner London Probation Service (1994b), *The Resident Speaks*, Inner London Probation Service, London.

Jamous, H. and Peloille, B. (1970), 'Professions or Self-Perpetuating Systems', in Jackson, J. (ed), *Professions and Professionalisation*, Cambridge University Press, Cambridge.

Jones, M., Mordecai, M., Rutter, F. and Thomas, L. (1993), 'The Miskin Model of Groupwork with Women Offenders', in Brown, A. and Caddick, B. (eds), *Groupwork with Offenders*, Whiting and Birch Ltd., London.

Kemshall, H. (1995), 'Risk In Probation Practice: The Hazards and Dangers of Supervision', *Probation Journal*, vol. 42, pp.67-72.

Kemshall, H. (1996), 'Risk Assessment: Fuzzy Thinking or 'Decisions in Action'?', *Probation Journal*, vol. 43, pp.2-7.

Kemshall, H. (1998), *Risk in Probation Practice*, Ashgate, Aldershot.

Kemshall, H. and Maguire, M. (2000), 'Public Protection, Partnership and Risk Penality', *Punishment and Society*, vol. 3, pp.237-64.

Kennedy, H. (1992), *Eve was Framed*, Vintage, London.

King, R. (2000), 'Doing Research in Prisons', in King, R. and Wincup, E. (eds), *Doing Research on Crime and Justice*, Oxford University Press, Oxford.

Langan, M. (1992), 'Introduction: Women and Social Work in the 1990s', in Langan, M. and Day, L. (eds) (1992), *Women, Oppression and Social Work*, Routledge, London.

Langan, M. and Day, L. (eds) (1992), *Women, Oppression and Social Work*, Routledge, London.

Lazarus, R. and Folkman, S. (1984), *Stress, Appraisal and Coping*, Springer Publishing Co., New York.

Leather, P., Cox, T. and Farnsworth, B. (1990), 'Violence at Work: An Issue for the 1990s', *Work and Stress*, vol. 4, pp.3-5.

Lewis, H. and Mair, G. (1989), *Bail and Probation Work II: The Use of London Probation/Bail Hostels for Bailees*, Home Office, London.

Light, R. (1993), 'Why Support Prisoners' Family Tie Groups?', *Howard Journal*, vol. 32, pp. 322-29.

Lipsky, M. (1988), *Street-level Bureaucracy: Dilemmas of the Individual in Public Services*, Russell Sage Foundation, New York.

Lloyd, C. (1986), *Response to SNOP*, Institute of Criminology, Cambridge.

Lloyd, C., Mair, G. and Hough, M. (1994), *Explaining Reconviction Rates: A Critical Analysis*, Home Office, London.

Lofland, J. and Lofland, L. (1984), *Analysing Social Settings*, Wadsworth, Belmont, Ca.

Loseke, D. (1989), 'Evaluation Research and the Practice of the Social Services', *Journal of Contemporary Ethnography*, vol. 18, pp.202-23.

Loseke, D. (1992), *The Battered Woman and Shelters: The Social Construction of Wife Abuse*, State University of New York Press, Albany.

McGuire, J. (1995) (eds) *What Works: Reducing Reoffending*, John Wiley, Chicester.

McLaughlin, E. and Muncie, J. (1994), 'Managing the Criminal Justice System', in Clarke, J., Cochrane, A. and McLaughlin, E. (eds), *Managing Social Policy*, Sage, London.

McLaughlin, E. and Muncie, J. (1996), 'Introduction' in McLaughlin, E. and Muncie, J. (eds), *Controlling Crime*, Sage, London.

Maguire, M. (1992), 'Parole', in Stockdale, E. and Casale, S. (eds), *Criminal Justice Under Stress*, Blackstone, London.

Mair, G. (2000), 'Research on Community Penalties', in King, R. and Wincup. E. (eds), *Doing Research on Crime and Justice*, Oxford University Press, Oxford.

Mair, G., Lloyd, C., Nee, C. and Sibbit, R. (1994), *Intensive Probation in England and Wales: An Evaluation*, Home Office Research Study 133, Home Office, London.

Marshall, C. and Rossman, G. (1989), *Designing Qualitative Research*, Sage, Newbury Park, Ca.

Martinson, R. (1974), 'What Works?', *The Public Interest*, March, pp.22-54.

Maslach, C. (1980), *Burnout: The Cost of Caring*, Prentice Hall, Englewood Cliffs.

Mathieson, D. (1992), 'The Probation Service', in E. Stockdale and S. Casale (eds) *Criminal Justice Under Stress*, Blackstone, London.

May, T. (1991), *Probation: Politics, Policy and Practice*, Open University Press, Buckingham.

Merchant, D. (1993), 'Gender: A Management Perspective', in Senior, P. and. Willliams, B. (eds), *Values, Gender and Offending*, PAVIC, Sheffield.

Messerschmidt, J. (1993), *Masculinities and Crime*, Rowman and Littlefield, Ottowa, NJ.

Miller, D. (2000), *Dying to Care?: Work, Stress and Burnout in HIV/AIDS Care*, Routledge, London.

Miller, S. (1970), *Prescription for Leadership: Training for the Medical Elite*, Aldine, Chicago.

Minogue, R. (1994), 'Women, Stereotypes and Court Reports', *Criminal Justice*, vol. 12, pp.3-5.

185

Mistry, T. (1993), 'Establishing a Feminist Model of Groupwork in the Probation Service', in Brown, A. and Caddick, B. (eds) *Groupwork with Offenders*, Whiting and Birch Ltd., London.

Morgan, R. (2000), 'The Politics of Criminological Research', in King, R. and Wincup, E. (eds), *Doing Research on Crime and Justice*, Oxford University Press, Oxford.

Morris, A., Wilkinson, C., Tisi, A., Woodrow, J. and Rockley, A. (1995), *Managing the Needs of Female Prisoners*, Home Office, London.

Morris, L. and Lyon, E. (eds) (1996), *Gender Relations in Public and Private*, Macmillan, Basingstoke.

Mulvie, C. (1993), 'Groupwork in the London Probation and Bail Hostel', in Brown, A. and Caddick, B. (eds) *Groupwork with Offenders*, Whiting and Birch Ltd., Luton.

NACRO (1995), *The Cost of Penal Measures*, NACRO Briefing 23, NACRO, London.

NAPO (2000), *Probation Directory 2000*, Shaw and Sons Ltd, Crayford.

National Audit Office (1989), *Home Office: Control and Management of Probation Services in England and Wales*, National Audit Office, London.

Newburn, T. (1995), *Crime and Criminal Justice Policy*, Longman, London.

Newburn, T. and Mair, G. (eds) (1996), *Working with Men*, Russell House Publishing, Lyme Regis.

Osler, A. (1995), *An Introduction to the Probation Service*, Waterside Press, Winchester.

Ostell, A. and Oakland, S. (1995), *Headteacher Stress, Coping and Health*, Avebury, Aldershot.

Otto, S. and Orford, J. (1978), *Not Quite Like Home: Small Hostels for Alcoholics and Others*, Wiley, Chicester.

Palmer, S. (1979), 'Style and Regime in Probation Hostels', *Probation Journal*, vol. 26, pp. 89-91.

Paylor, I. (1995), *Housing Needs of Ex-Offenders*, Ashgate, Aldershot.

Payne, C. and Scott, T. (1982), *Developing Supervision of Team in Field and Residential Social Work*, National Institute of Social Work, London.

Payne, G. (1989), 'Bail Hostels: Between Bail and Jail', *Probation Journal*, vol. 39, pp.37-40.

Pearson, G. (1993), 'Talking a Good Fight: Authenticity and Distance in the Ethnographer's Craft', in Hobbs. D. and May, T. (eds),

Interpreting the Field: Accounts of Ethnography, Oxford University Press, Oxford.

Phillpots, G. and Lancucki, L. (1979), *Previous Convictions, Sentences and Reconvictions: A Statistical Study of a Sample of 5,000 Offenders Convicted in 1971*, Home Office, London.

Pines, A., Aronson, E. and Kafrey, D. (1981), *Burnout: From Tedium to Personal Growth*, Free Press, New York.

Pithouse, A. (1987), *Social Work: The Social Organisation of an Invisible Trade*, Gower, Aldershot.

Pithouse, A. (1994), 'The Happy Family: Learning Colleagueship in a Social Work Team', in Coffey, A. and Atkinson, P. (eds), *Occupational Socialisation and Working Lives*, Ashgate, Aldershot.

Pithouse, A. and Atkinson, P. (1988), 'Telling the Case: The Occupational Narrative in the Social Work Office', in Coupland, N. (ed), *Styles of Discourse*, Croom Helm, London.

Pitts, J. (1992), 'The End of an Era', *Howard Journal*, vol. 31, pp.133-48.

Poyner, B. and Warne, C. (1986), *Violence to Staff: A Basis for Assessment and Prevention*, Health and Safety Executive, London.

Pollert, A. (1981) *Girls, Wives and Factory Lives*, Macmillan, Basingstoke.

Pollner, M. (1987) *Mundane Reason*, Cambridge University Press, Cambridge.

Pratt, J. and Bray, K. (1985), 'Bail Hostels: Alternatives to Custody?', *British Journal of Criminology*, vol. 25, pp.160-71.

Prison Reform Trust (1999), *Prison Privatisation Report International*, issue 26, Prison Reform Trust, London.

Raynor, P. and Vanstone, M. (1994), 'Probation Practice, Effectiveness and the Non-Treatment Paradigm', *British Journal of Social Work*, vol. 24, pp.387-404.

Rees, T. (1992), *Women and Labour Market*, Routledge, London.

Reiner, R. (2000), *The Politics of the Police*, Oxford University Press, Oxford.

Reinharz, S. (1992), *Feminist Methods in Social Research*, Oxford University Press, New York.

Rock, P. (1979), 'Another Common-sense Conception of Deviancy', *Sociology*, vol. 13, pp.75-88.

Rumjay, J. (1996), 'Women Offenders: Towards Needs Based Policy', *Vista*, September pp.104-15.

187

Sapsed, C. (1993) 'Groups and Groupings in a Probation Hostel', in Brown, A. and Caddick, B. (eds), *Groupwork with Offenders*, Whiting and Birch Ltd., Luton.

Satyamurti, C. (1981), *Occupational Survival: The Case of Local Authority Social Workers*, Blackwell, Oxford.

Schatzman, L. and Strauss, A. (1973), *Field Research*, Prentice Hall, Englewoods Cliffs, NJ.

Schon, D. (1995), *The Reflective Practitioner*, Arena, Aldershot.

Schutz, A. (1967), *The Phenomenology of the Social World*, Northwestern University Press, Evanston.

SCODA (1996), *Through the Eye of a Needle: A Survey of Community Care Implementation and Drug Services*, SCODA, London.

Scourfield, J. (1998), 'Probation Officers: Working with Men', *British Journal of Social Work*, vol. 28, pp.581-99.

Shaw, I. (1996), *Evaluating in Practice*, Arena, Aldershot.

Shaw, I. and Shaw, A. (1999), 'Game Plans, Buzzes and Sheer Luck: Doing Well in Social Work', in S. Kirk (ed), *Social Work Research Methods*, NASW Press, Washington DC.

Simon, F. and Wilson, R. (1976), *Field Wing Bail Hostel: The First Nine Months*, Home Office Research Study No. 30, London, Home Office.

Sinclair, I. (1979), *Hostels for Probationers*, Home Office Research Study No. 6, Home Office, London.

Smith, C. and Wincup, E. (2000), 'Breaking In: Researching Criminal Justice Institutions for Women', in King, R. and Wincup. E. (eds), *Doing Research on Crime and Justice,* Oxford University Press, Oxford.

Smith, F. and Wilson, S. (1975), *Field Wing Bail Hostel: The First Nine Months*, Home Office, London.

Sparks, R. (1996), 'Prisons, Punishment and Penality', in McLaughlin, E. and Muncie, J. (eds), *Controlling Crime*, Sage, London.

Stevenson, D. and Parsloe, P. (1978), *Social Work Teams: The Practitioner's View*, HMSO, London.

Stewart, G. (1996), 'Housing', in Drakeford, M. and Vanstone, M. (eds), *Beyond Offending Behaviour*, Ashgate, Aldershot.

Stewart, J., Smith, D., Stewart, G. with Fullwood, C. (1994), *Understanding Offending Behaviour*, Longman, Harlow.

Tallant, C. and Strachan, R. (1995), 'The Importance of Framing: A Pragmatic Approach to Risk Assessment', *Probation Journal*, vol. 42, pp.215-20.

Thomas, L. (1993), 'Groupwork with Women Offenders: A Source of Empowerment for Users, Workers and Agency', in Brown, A. and Caddick, B. (eds), *Groupwork with Offenders*, Whiting and Birch Ltd., London.

Todd, M. (1996), *Opening Doors: An Evaluation of the Cultural Sensitivity of Offender Hostel Provision in Greater Manchester*, Greater Manchester Probation Service, Manchester.

Underdown, A. (1998), *Strategies for Effective Offender Supervision*, Home Office, London.

Vennard, J., Sugg, D. and Hedderman, C. (1997), *Changing Offenders' Attitudes and Behaviour, What Works?*, Home Office Research Study 171, Home Office, London.

Walby, S. and Greenwell, J. (1994) 'Managing the National Health Service', in Clarke, J. Cochrane, A. and McLaughlin, E. (eds), *Managing Social Policy*, Sage, London.

Walker, H. (1985), 'Women's Issues in Probation Practice', in Walker, H. and. Beaumont, B. (eds), *Working with Offenders*, Macmillan, London.

Waterhouse, J. (2000), 'The Future of Scottish National Standards', *Probation Journal*, vol. 47, pp.56-58.

Watson, F. (1994), 'Success or Failure? Outcomes of Bailees at Hope House Hostel', *British Journal of Social Work*, vol. 24, pp.597-616.

Watson, T. (1995), *Sociology, Work and Industry*, Routledge: London.

Westwood, S. (1984), *All Day Every Day: Factory and Family in the Making of Women's Lives*, Pluto Press, London.

White, K. and Brody, S. (1980), 'The Use of Bail Hostels', *Criminal Law Review*, pp. 420-25.

Wincup, E. (1996), 'Mixed Hostels: Staff and Resident Perspectives', *Probation Journal*, vol. 43, pp.147-51.

Wincup, E. (1997), *Waiting for Trial: Living and Working in a Bail Hostel*, Unpublished PhD thesis, Cardiff University.

Wincup, E. (1998), 'Power, Control and the Gendered Body' in Richardson, J. and Shaw, A. (eds), *The Body in Qualitative Research*, Ashgate, Aldershot.

Wincup, E. (1999a), 'Women Awaiting Trial: Common Problems and Coping Strategies', *The British Criminology Conferences: Selected Proceedings*, vol.2,
http://www.lboro.ac.uk/departments/ss/bsc/bsccp/vol02/Vol02.html.

Wincup, E. (1999b), 'Researching Women Awaiting Trial: Dilemmas of Feminist Ethnography', in Brookman, F., Noaks, L. and Wincup, E. (eds), *Qualitative Research in Criminology,* Ashgate, Aldershot.

Wincup, E. (2000), 'Surviving Through Substance Use: The Role of Substances in the Lives of Women who Appear Before the Courts' *Sociological Research On-Line*, vol. 4,
http://www.socresonline.org.uk.

Wincup, E. (2001a), 'Managing Security in Semi-Penal Institutions for Women', *Security Journal*, vol. 14, pp.41-51.

Wincup, E. (2001b), 'Feminist Research with Women Awaiting Trial: The Effects on Participants in the Qualitative Research Process', in Gilbert, K. (ed), *The Emotional Nature of Qualitative Research*, CRC Press, Florida.

Wincup, E., Maguire, M., Bayliss, R., Tanner, C. and Wood, F. (1998), *Review of Purchasing Requirements for, and Provision of, Drug and Alcohol Residential Community Facilities in Wales*, Cardiff University, Cardiff.

Woolf, Lord Justice (1991), *Prison Disturbances April 1990: Report of an Inquiry by the Rt Hon Lord Justice Woolf (Parts I and II) and His Honour Judge Stephen Tumim (Part II)*, Home Office, London.

Worrall, A. (1995), 'Justice Through Inequality? The Probation Service and Women Offenders', in Ward, D. and Lacey, M. (eds) *Probation: Working for Justice*, Whiting and Birch, London.

Worrall, A. (1997a), *Punishment in the Community*, Longman, London.

Worrall, A. (1997b), *Community Punishment 2000: At Liberty to Kill and Rape?*, Paper presented to the 1997 British Criminology Conference, Belfast, July.

Worrall, A. (1998), 'Real Punishment for Real Criminals? Community Sentences and the Gendering of Punishment', *British Criminology Conference Selected Proceedings*, vol. 1,
http:www.lboro.ac.uk/departments/ss/bsc/bccsp/vol01/vo101.HTM.

Worrall, A. (2000), 'Community Sentences for Women: Where have they gone?', *Criminal Justice Matters*, no.39, pp.10-11.

Worrall, A. (2001), 'Girls at Risk? Reflections on Changing Attitudes to Young Women's Offending', *Probation Journal*, vol. 48, pp.86-92.

Wright, A. and Davies, M. (1989), *Becoming a Probation Officer*, University of East Anglia Social Work Monographs, Norwich.
Wright, L. and Kemshall, H. (1994), 'Feminist Probation Practice: Making Supervision Meaningful', *Probation Journal*, vol. 41, pp.73-80.